Trends in World Politics

Bruce M. Russett

The Macmillan Company, New York
Collier–Macmillan Limited, London

Much of this book draws upon research I have done previously and on ideas that have developed over the past several years. Colleagues at Yale, M.I.T., and elsewhere have contributed in essential ways to the book's intellectual input. Hayward Alker and Karl Deutsch deserve particular mention. The research has been generously supported by grants from the National Science Foundation and the Social Science Research Council. For their help in the physical preparation of this volume I must express my thanks to Kay A. Latona, who carefully prepared the manuscript, and to Norman Hix, who drew the graphs. Portions of Chapter 4 appeared previously in my article entitled, "Toward a Model of Competitive International Politics," Journal of Politics, *XXV, 2 (May 1963), pp. 226–247, and parts of Chapter 8 appeared in Bruce M. Russett* et al., World Handbook of Political and Social Indicators *(New Haven, Conn.: Yale University Press, 1964). Both are reprinted with permission.*

BRUCE M. RUSSETT

Fourth Printing, 1967

Library of Congress catalog card number: 65–15171

THE MACMILLAN COMPANY, NEW YORK
COLLIER–MACMILLAN CANADA, LTD., TORONTO, ONTARIO

PRINTED IN THE UNITED STATES OF AMERICA

Preface

In this book I have tried to achieve two goals. First, the volume represents an attempt to assess some of the changes in the international political system during this century, especially changes since 1945, and their possible consequences for the future. Every observer of the world situation is aware that in some sense, to some degree, the international system is changing. The superpowers' confrontation does not dominate world politics quite as much as it did. Western Europe is not as dependent upon the United States, either economically or strategically, as it was a decade or two ago. Hostility between Communist China and the Soviet Union has increased well above the level predicted by most students of the Communist bloc even at the end of the 1950's. In the United Nations the conflict between former colonies and former colonial powers is at least as important as Cold War differences.

To say that changes are appearing in the pattern of international relations with which we have been familiar is not to assert dogmatically that those changes are or will be revolutionary. I do not, for example, believe that we are on the verge of a "new balance of power," a world state, or any such drastic transformation. But without examining developments with some care, we have no right to assume that international politics will continue precisely as usual—which I believe they will not do. Thus this book examines the following trends: (1) the transformation of the international environment by the mushrooming growth of science and capabilities for transportation, communication, and destruction; (2) recent and projected trends in North Atlantic integration, specifically whether that integration may be limited to the Common Market countries or encompass a wider area; (3) changes in the United Nations, including the rising influence of the neutrals; (4) the demands of many poor countries for faster economic development, and the probable effects of those demands on the international system as a whole, especially the probability that a major have-not power will arise to challenge the West and the Soviets; (5) some recent developments in the Sino–Soviet relationship.

The second aim of the book is to introduce the reader to a variety of techniques for the empirical analysis of international relations. I wrote the volume intending to show, in the context of substantive discussion of important problems, how several kinds of simple quantitative data can be used to describe the world of international politics and to test hypotheses.

BRUCE M. RUSSETT

Contents

CHAPTER 1

Evolution and Revolution in International Society

The Balance of Power Precarious

IN 1914 THERE WERE eight countries that in some degree or other might have been described as "great powers": Britain, France, Germany, Italy, Austria–Hungary, and Russia in Europe, the United States, and emergent Japan in Asia. Russia, the largest, had about four times the population of Italy, France, or Britain, but all the latter, especially France and Britain, were far more industrialized and had huge colonial empires. Of the eight nations the United States was potentially the most powerful, but its geographical isolation kept it outside the main arena of competition. There were of course important differences in size, military capability, economic development, and internal cohesion among the powers, but to a substantial degree a nation's weakness in one was compensated by strength in another. In short, the system was composed of relative equals, making possible a "balance-of-power system."

But a balance-of-power system requires flexibility and balancing. To the degree that one power or a coalition of powers becomes predominant, or the alignments coalesce into confronting alliances, the system undergoes major change. On the eve of World War I two rival coalitions faced each other in Europe: the Triple Alliance (Germany, Austria, and Italy) and the Triple Entente (Britain, France, and Russia). The other major powers, Japan and the United States, were far from the chief zone of confrontation. In 1914 the system was not quite as rigid as it might appear from this roster. Germany and Austria were tightly allied, but neither fully trusted Italy to fight on its side (and rightly). Likewise France and Russia could depend upon each other, but were sure of no more than neutrality from England in the event of major war. Uncertainty about the behavior of allies, and uncertainty about each other's actual military capabilities, mitigated against any very sure estimates of relative strength or confident predictions about the outcome of crisis. In any case all powers shared important interests in maintaining the system as it was. All had colonial empires of some size (Austria's and Russia's were adjacent to their home territory), and by the strength of their predominance over the small powers of the world they supported and were supported by a common system of finance, international law, culture, and morality. They were aware of their competitive interests, but also of those they shared. The system was dangerously unstable, but the remnants of an ordered, predictable, and basically pacific system remained.

The year 1914 marks the last year of what could by any stretch of semantics be called a stable balance-of-power system. 1918 ushered in what can at best be termed "the balance of power precarious." One of the major powers of 1914, Austria–Hungary, was totally dismembered. War, economic collapse, and very unfavorable peace treaties left prostrate two other major powers, Germany and Russia. Forced disarmament and further economic chaos kept Germany relatively powerless for two more decades; civil war and social revolution did the same for Russia. The Versailles peace treaty made reciprocal the hatred Frenchmen had previously borne for Germans, and Soviet Russia received and returned with interest the hostility of the capitalist world. Several of the remaining powers—Britain, France, and the United States—were so disillusioned with what their victory had wrought that their willingness to use force to restrain future challenges was seriously weakened. With the reduction in the number of great powers and the deep bitterness dividing those that were left, the balance-of-power system could never be the same. Its essential condition—flexibility—was lost. When Nazi Germany made its bid to dominate the system, the nature of its challenge was not recognized until very nearly too late.

A Bipolar World

If 1918–1939 may be described as exemplifying "the balance of power precarious," the post-1945 world marked a totally new system. It was, and remains, essentially a bipolar system. The extent of that bipolarity, implying a major gap between the strength of the two superpowers and those of the next rank, can be seen by examining their relative Gross National Products (G.N.P.). G.N.P. is the best summary measure of national power that we have. It combines both a nation's size and its level of economic development in a figure for the total value of goods produced. Though it does not show the *kind* of goods produced, it measures the total productive capacity of the economy, and in time the use of that capacity can be shifted from one good to another.[1] China, because of its huge population, ranks far above other poor states like Burma and Pakistan, but because of its low level of economic development nevertheless ranks well below such advanced but smaller countries as the United States and Russia.

G.N.P. is not a perfect measure of power, however, primarily because it cannot indicate differences in the internal distribution of resources, or in the tightness of domestic political control. The Soviet Union, for instance, is more powerful than its G.N.P. would indicate, because it is able, with its totalitarian system, to enforce a low level of consumption on its populace and turn the "savings" into investment in heavy industry and military equipment. Thus a strict comparison of G.N.P.'s would exaggerate the gap between the United States and its major current antagonist, and at the same time would underestimate the gap between Russia and the major European states. And in the 1930's both China and Russia were probably weaker than their G.N.P.'s would suggest, because large segments of the population of both, especially China, were hostile to their governments and engaged in more or less active revolt.[2] But useful comparisons of countries are possible so long as we remember that we are dealing with rough orders of magnitude rather than with precise figures. Table 1.1 gives the broad picture for relative world power in 1938, 1950, and 1963. We use an index which equates the G.N.P. of the United States at each time with 100, and expresses other countries' G.N.P.'s as a percentage of America's.

The difference between the world before and after World War II

[1] See A. F. K. Organski, *World Politics* (New York: Alfred A. Knopf, 1958), Chs. 5–8, and Charles J. Hitch and Dayton McKean, *The Economics of Defense in the Nuclear Age* (Cambridge, Mass.: Harvard University Press, 1960), Ch. 1.

[2] Another problem that often hinders the creation of a reasonably accurate index of national power stems from the comparison of goods produced in countries with different currencies and price structures. Radios, for instance, may be at least as expensive in Burma as in America, but rice is very much cheaper. And the Burmese produce far more rice than radios. So if we compare the G.N.P. of Burma with that of the United States in American prices, Burma looks very much richer than if we use Burmese prices, which, for comparative purposes, do less than justice to the value of Burma's rice production. On the other hand, American prices also distort the "true" picture. What is needed is some combination of the two into "standard" prices, and this is a very demanding task, made more difficult when we try to compare the product of free enterprise economies with that of Communist states. The figures in Table 1.1 give a rough estimate of G.N.P. in standardized prices.

Table 1.1 **Indices of Relative G.N.P., in Standard Prices, for Six Major Powers (U.S. = 100)**

	G.N.P. Index		
	1938	*1950*	*1963*
United States	100	100	100
Russia	47	34	49
Germany	34	13	19
Great Britain	30	19	16
France	24	15	18
China	24	18	20

SOURCES:

China: Ta-chung Liu and Kung-chia Yeh, *The Economy of the Chinese Mainland: National Income and Economic Development* (Santa Monica, Calif.: The RAND Corporation, 1963), p. 94, adjusted to standard prices from data in Alexander Eckstein, *The National Income of Communist China* (New York: The Free Press, 1961), p. 69. Growth rate since 1959 is estimated. Data in columns for 1938 and 1950 actually are for 1933 and 1952.

All others: 1960 estimates, in standard prices, from Stanley Cohn, "The Gross National Product in the Soviet Union: Comparative Growth Rates," *Dimensions of Soviet Economic Power,* Studies Prepared for the Joint Economic Committee, 87th Congress, 2d Session, Washington, 1962, p. 76. Earlier years calculated from growth rates in D. C. Paige, "Economic Growth: The Last Hundred Years," *National Institute Economic Review* (July 1961), p. 49, and Abram Bergson, "National Income," in Abram Bergson and Simon Kuznets, *Economic Trends in the Soviet Union* (Cambridge, Mass.: Harvard University Press, 1963), p. 6. Growth rates since 1960 from *Federal Reserve Bulletin,* January 1964, p. 104 (U.S.), and U.N., *Economic Survey of Europe, 1962,* Geneva, 1963, I, Ch. 1, p. 2, and Ch. 2, p. 3. "Germany" in 1938 includes eastern territories and Austria; later years, Federal Republic only.

is striking. In 1938 the United States was more than twice as "powerful" as any other country, but technology was still sufficiently limited to keep her relatively isolated. Russia was second, but still beset by internal problems. Though Germany was probably the most powerful of the rest, the big countries of Western Europe were still of fairly equal strength, and some semblance of a balance-of-power system remained. For the whole range of six powers the strongest, America, was only four times more productive than the weakest and only three times more productive than the third-ranking country, Germany. But after the European countries had bled each other in World War II America was five times as productive as the number-three country (then Britain) and almost eight times as strong as a divided and war-torn Germany (West Germany only). Russia, though weakened relative to the United States, was then almost twice as strong as her nearest challenger, Great Britain. It is this widened distance between the second- and third-ranking powers that we most often mean when we speak of a bipolar world.

The increased gap between the greatest powers and those on the next level was made even greater when all of Europe's major colonies achieved their independence. A colony is by no means always an asset, and it is almost never as valuable as an equivalent population or piece of territory within the mother country. But as long as it is politically quiescent it usually makes some contribution to the colonial power's strength. If its resources are properly developed, it can make important supplements to the colonial power's economy, and the colony may provide for service elsewhere at least as many troops as it ties down. India, for example, made a significant military and economic contribution to the British war effort in World War I. In both wars France made fairly extensive use of African troops in Europe.

Britain suffered most by the loss of her colonies. By the late 1950's virtually all of her former empire was gone; since World War II independence had been achieved by countries with a population over ten times her own and with a combined G.N.P. of at least two thirds of Britain's. France had lost the rich area of Indo-China, Morocco and Tunisia had become independent, and a long and costly war made far-from-quiescent Algeria a major net liability. The most important parts of the Japanese Empire were acquired in the decades before World War II, and their acquisition helped embolden the Japanese to attempt further expansion. In 1945 the Japanese lost industrially significant Manchuria and Korea, Taiwan, and other valuable island possessions. Only the United States and Russia emerged relatively unscathed. America lost the Philippines, but they represented less than a sixth of the American population and only a very small fraction of American G.N.P. Russia gained major bordering territories from Poland, Romania, Czechoslovakia, Finland, Germany, and Japan, and swallowed whole the Baltic states of Estonia, Latvia, and Lithuania.

One more major factor contributed to the overweening position of the two great continental powers: atomic energy. The United States achieved a major military breakthrough with the atomic bomb in 1945; it had a weapon which could destroy the war-making capacities of any other power.[3] Publicly the Soviet Union deprecated the value of this revolutionary development; privately it embarked on a crash program to produce its own atomic bomb, which it succeeded in doing in 1949. The Soviets actually preceded, by a few months, the United

[3] Though not necessarily before the other power could do enormous damage in retaliation against American allies. In the late 1940's the United States certainly could have defeated the Russians; it almost as certainly could not have prevented the devastation of Western Europe by Soviet land forces.

States in the creation of a workable hydrogen bomb. Five years later Britain followed, and later France and China joined the nuclear powers. But Britain's nuclear force has never been of a quality or size at all comparable with that of the great powers, France's is still weaker, and China's is trivial. It is virtually impossible for any but the largest industrial power to build a force of sophisticated delivery vehicles capable of representing an *offensive* threat against the United States or Russia. Possibly a smaller nation can produce a "minimum deterrent," that is, a force that can deter direct thermonuclear attack upon itself, but even that is open to some doubt.

In this postwar world of superpowers, lost colonies, and thermonuclear weapons, the United States was temporarily preponderant, though not dominant. For a while its G.N.P. was three times the size of Russia's. It had the ability to prevent Soviet expansion into Western Europe or the rimlands of Asia, but geographical distance and a weakness in ground forces meant that it could only have rolled back the Russians at great cost to itself and immense cost to its European friends. By the late 1950's this preponderance diminished as the Soviets recovered rapidly from World War II and built nuclear weapons. But in any case these two powers were clearly preponderant over the rest of the world. For their security even such proud and once powerful nations as Britain and France were utterly dependent upon American guarantees. Without the United States' promise of help Western Europe could not have defended itself, as all parties concerned were aware. And Communist regimes could be maintained in the Soviet Satellites only through the use or threat of Russian military might. The Chinese Communist regime, for instance, would almost certainly have been overthrown with active American aid except for the virtual certainty that any such effort would quickly have involved the U.S.S.R. The American system of military alliances embraced 43 nations and over a third of the world's population; the Soviet Bloc included 12 countries and another third of the globe's inhabitants. The "neutral bloc" was hardly a bloc. Though it had just a little less than a third of the population of the world, the "neutral" states without exception were either small or poor and seemed often to have little in common beyond their desire somehow to avoid the great-power struggle. In short, this was truly a bipolar world: two major nations, with their dependent allies, confronting each other and between them including most of the militarily significant areas of the earth.

The Exponential Growth of Science and Technology

It was a bipolar world in a way that had never before been possible—the world was a single, close-knit system, with all peoples bound inextricably together by facilities for the rapid transport of men, messages, and weapons, by enormously expanded destructive capabilities, and by the rapid advance of science in so many fields. What happened in the middle of the twentieth century was not *merely* a continuation in the accretion of scientific and technological advance that had been maintained for several hundred years. Though change continued at the exponential *rates* established earlier, the effects were truly revolutionary. Four graphs will help describe both the continuity and the change implied by recent developments.

The first of these graphs shows what has happened in transportation since the early nineteenth century. It gives the maximum speed of human transportation over intercontinental distances. Figure 1.1 begins with sailing vessels and the earliest steamships, shows roughly the maximum speed attained by oceangoing passenger ships in the period between the First and Second World Wars, and then the rapid advance made by long-range aircraft, culminating in bombers of the 1960's that travel at well over the speed of sound. At first the improvement in transportation was fairly slow, but by the middle of this century changes were taking place extremely rapidly.

But it is misleading to place too much emphasis on the rapidity of current change. Actually the *rates* of change have been rather steady over this whole period. Essentially what the curve shows is an exponential growth rate, a squaring of the maximum speed about every 60 years, beginning around 1830. Sailing ships could consistently do only about five miles per hour at that time, and the early steamships were hardly better. But before the end of the century steamships were good for 25 miles per hour; air speeds of over 600 miles an hour were reached by the 1950's. The fit of this growth rate is not perfect—it was actually slowed down between the perfection of the steamship and the advent of long-range aircraft, and has been a little faster since, but the general outlines are there. The perfection of man-carrying rockets, traveling at around 20,000 miles per hour, can be seen as an extension of this very trend.

Now we have not explained the causes of this trend, and without doing so have no right to project it into the future. Nevertheless, the

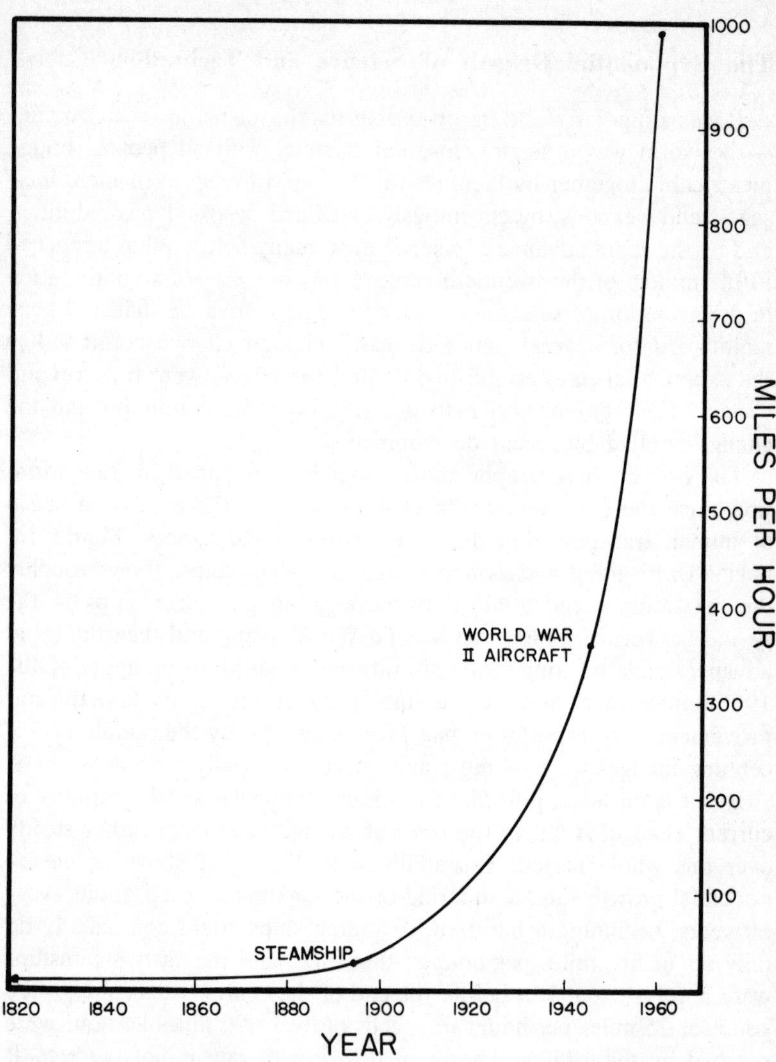

FIGURE 1.1 A shrinking world: Maximum speed attainable for travel over intercontinental distances, 1820–1960.

fact that it has existed over the past century and a half has had enormous consequences for international relations. While travel was still confined to the lower speeds, the consequences were not so dramatic or perhaps even so serious, but more recently the change has meant the irrevocable binding of the whole world into a closely knit system. America's privileged geographical asset, her isolation that in part made it possible for more than 100 years to avoid becoming enmeshed in Europe's wars, slipped away slowly and without much notice for a long time. But within the past few decades, as the exponential rate was operating on higher transportation speeds, the change became unmistakable. What happens in Africa or Asia may affect us immediately, and we are within military reach of hostile European or Asian powers. Furthermore, it has implied the extension of our own power. The balance of power system could operate after a fashion, even as late as the 1930's, despite the unchallenged first position America held in G.N.P. Distance made the exercise of our power outside the Western Hemisphere both difficult and expensive; it was an equalizer that nullified some of the power that our huge economy seemed to convey. Thus the end of our isolation has meant not only that others could affect us in ways once impossible, but also that we can exercise our power in regions which not too long ago were beyond the economical use of our strength. And the same is true of the Russians, when both of us bring our power to bear in Southeast Asia or the Middle East.

A similar trend has taken place in the destructive capacity of explosive weapons. Sometimes the growth in explosive power is used to dramatize the change, but that is deceptive, for doubling the bang does not double the area destroyed. (Actually it only increases it by about 57 per cent.) And there is no need to exaggerate the effects, for they are impressive enough. Figure 1.2 shows the increase in the radius of destruction of a single weapon, beginning with artillery shells during the Civil War and continuing through the guns of the turn of the century, the largest conventional bombs dropped in World War II, and the thermonuclear weapons of the present.

Again the measurements are rough, but the general picture is clear. Until the end of World War II the radius of destruction seems to have grown at a rate of about tenfold every 40 years, or an exponential rate of $\log^{10}$ for about 40 years. But the atomic bomb, when dropped on Hiroshima, expanded man's destructive capabilities in an absolutely unprecedented manner. The best of the World War II "blockbusters" could seriously damage only those buildings within about 500 feet (a tenth of a mile), but the atomic bomb destroyed most buildings within over a mile and a half. More recent scientific developments have raised this very substantially, to about 30 miles with the Soviet 100 megaton weapon, and they have achieved this twentyfold increase not in 80 years but in less than 20. The difference is such as

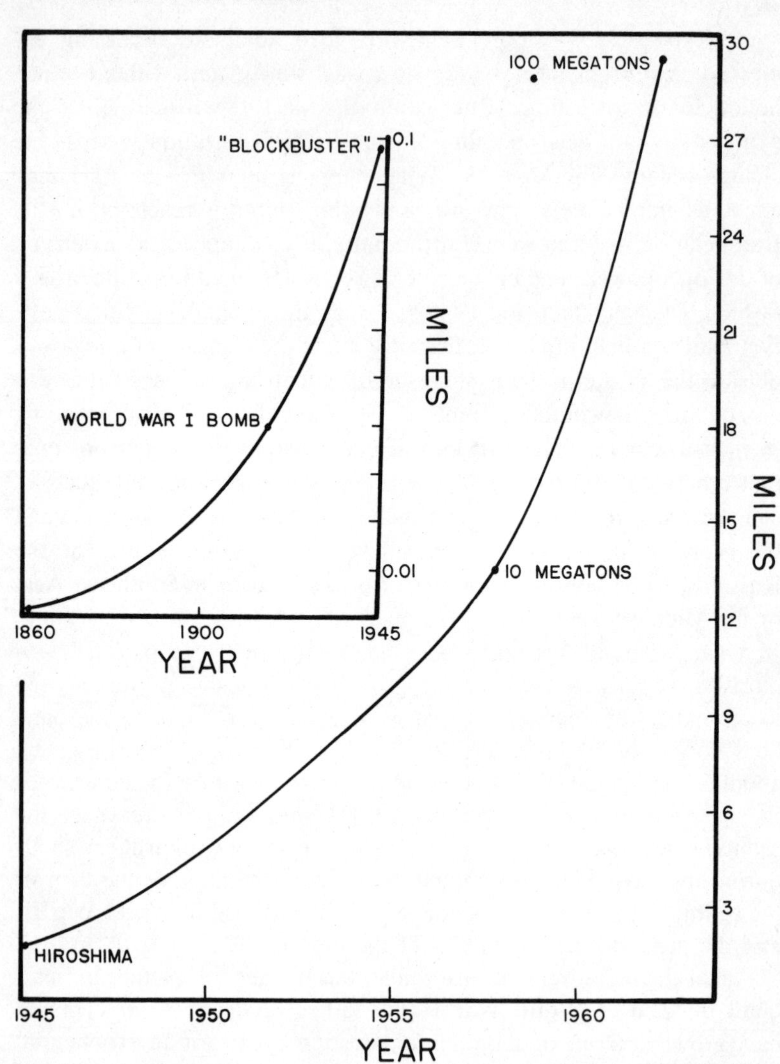

FIGURE 1.2 More bang for a bomb: Maximum destructive radius of existing weapons, 1860–1960. *(Calculated from U.S. Atomic Energy Commission,* The Effects of Nuclear Weapons *(Washington, 1962). Destructive radius defined as sufficient blast overpressure (3 pounds per square inch) to collapse an ordinary frame house.)*

to require us to use two graphs to show both the old trend and the new one as it was introduced with the nuclear age. It would have been alarming enough if man's destructive capacity had continued only to grow at the original rate, but with the jump the consequences are even more far-reaching. In the late 1960's man lives in a world of far greater interdependence and far greater capability than was true only two decades ago.

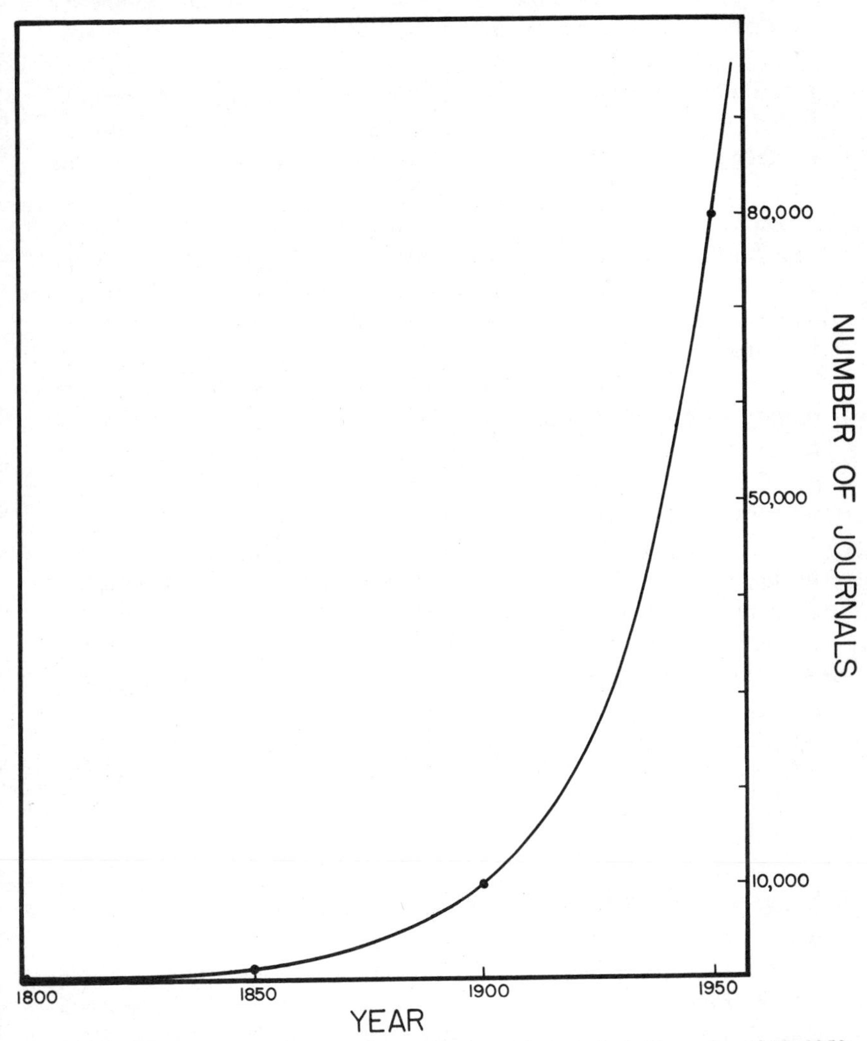

FIGURE 1.3 The scientific explosion: Number of technical journals, 1800–1950. *(Source: Derek J. DeSolla Price,* Science Since Babylon *(New Haven, Conn., 1961), p. 97.)*

Figure 1.3 illustrates one of the forces behind the growth rates shown in the first two graphs—the expansion of science. Scientists publish papers so that their colleagues will know what they have accomplished, and the frequency with which individual scientists publish papers is remarkably constant. A few great researchers publish hundreds of papers, while others produce only one or none at all, yet over time, and from one country to another, the average is quite steady. Thus a general approximation of the total number of scientists working at any one time is provided by the number of papers being published or even, without introducing much additional error, by the number of scientific and technical journals in existence throughout the world.

The scientific establishment has also grown enormously. Again the rate is a logarithmic one, this time of a tenfold increase about every 50 years. Whereas there were only about 100 journals in 1800, the figure grew to around 1000 in 1850, 10,000 in 1900, and not much less than 100,000 in the middle of the twentieth century. This itself is merely a continuation of a trend that can be traced back to the end of the seventeenth century. A close look at the growth rates, while remembering that one thing they indicate is the number of men engaged in scientific research, stimulates this observation: of all the scientists who *ever* lived, 90 per cent are alive *today*.

The world has contracted, destructive potential has expanded, and science has burgeoned. Partly as a consequence of these technological developments, and partly as an independent result of political change, the number of deaths from war has increased. War is of course a phenomenon as old as organized society, but its scope has become greater in recent years. There have been fewer major wars in the last couple of centuries, but those that have occurred have involved far more people than ever before. Man has mastered his environment so that he has unprecedented means to deliver destruction anywhere, and he has done so. Figure 1.4 shows the number of people who died, whether in action or from disease, in major wars for three periods since 1820. Major wars are considered to be all conflicts involving at least 500 deaths.

Once more we see a very sharp increase. Less than 2 million people died in wars between 1820 and 1863.[4] From 1864 to 1907 about 4.5 million died in wars, and over 40 million in the final period. Very roughly this also is equivalent to a tenfold increase every 50 years, though the rate seems to be slightly higher for recent years than for

[4] Extending the series back to the Napoleonic Wars (c. 1800) would raise the first point somewhat, though probably not above that now given for 1864–1907.

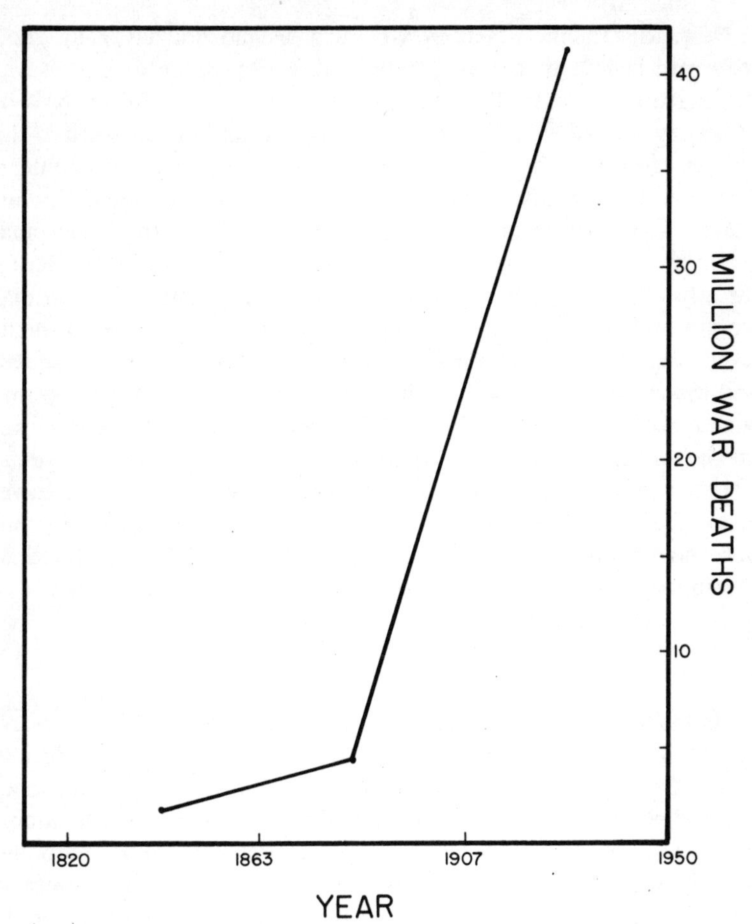

FIGURE 1.4 Conflict becomes global: Deaths from all wars involving 500 or more deaths; 1820–1863, 1863–1907, 1907–1950. *(Adapted from a compilation by Herbert K. Weiss, "Trends in World Involvement in War," Table 2 (mimeo.). Data originally collected by Lewis F. Richardson,* Statistics of Deadly Quarrels *(Chicago and Pittsburgh, 1960.) All deaths from the American Civil War are counted as in the first period.)*

earlier ones. Interestingly there is no increase in the number of wars over time—each of our periods is marked by about 100 conflicts. The difference is in size, for each World War killed about ten times as many people as did any previous war. If this growth rate of tenfold about every 50 years were to continue, wars by around the end of this century would kill the equivalent of the present population of the globe.

Now, as with the other growth rates, we do not have any good reason to believe that deaths from wars will continue to increase as they have in the past. To project a trend requires careful analysis of its causes, and all we intend here is to show what has happened in the past and to set out current world problems in their historical context. Some of these trends, in fact, simply cannot continue long. For instance, about one fifth of all Americans who have the intellectual capacity to become distinguished scientists in fact do so. Considering the other kinds of positions open to these gifted people, it is clear that we are now not far from scraping the bottom of the barrel of high-level scientific manpower.[5] The saturation point is nearly reached, and the trend *must* level off. Similarly, no matter how impressed one is with recent technological accomplishments it is hard to believe that maximum travel speed will continue to be squared every 70 years. If that were to happen man would, before a century passed, travel faster than the speed of light—and some science fiction aside, that does not seem likely. But such explosive change is not required to revolutionize world politics; more modest increases have sufficed.

A Loosened Bipolarity

As the background conditions have evolved rapidly in recent years, the political system too has changed from what it was only a decade and a half ago. Not all these changes can yet be clearly divined. (Actually, given the rapidity of change in the background conditions, who would expect our perception of political changes to be sharp and clear immediately?) In attempting to describe it we still deal more in tendencies whose outlines are vague and may be reversed than we do in easily identifiable trends. Yet tendencies there are.

First is the narrowing of the gap between the two major powers, the diminution in American predominance. In the 13 years following 1950 the Soviet Union's G.N.P. moved up from one third to one half of America's. Russia is now better able to spare scarce resources for military research and development, aid to the developing countries, and even occasional sops to her still hard-pressed consumers. Other countries too have closed a little of the gap separating them from the United States. Most striking is Communist China, which according to our rough estimates on page 4 has moved up to the number-three

[5] Derek J. De Solla Price, *Little Science, Big Science* (New York: Columbia University Press, 1963), p. 53.

position. But Germany and France too have improved their relative positions. Though they are hardly "superpowers," they are less inferior than they were just after the last war. A number of other countries not included in this table, such as the East European satellites, Japan, Italy, and other Western European states, have shown remarkable improvement in their relative economic position. And the United States' strength has been diminished in a way that does not show up in the G.N.P. table. Immediately after World War II America's balance of payments was extremely favorable because the world was full of markets for American goods. But when other nations recovered, this strength was lost and even turned into a gold outflow. With the drain on her balance of payments the United States reduced some of her overseas military commitments, her foreign investments, and some foreign economic and military aid. These reductions were not entirely costless to American foreign policy. Investments and troops abroad often serve in important ways to promote our national aims, and foreign aid is a key instrument for influencing people and governments (see Chapter 6).

Probably the most important changes, however, were military–political rather than economic. The old American guarantee of Western Europe's liberty no longer meant what it once did. In the early postwar years the United States could threaten to bomb Russia in response to any major attack on Europe. Because the Soviets lacked the means to retaliate effectively this threat was plausible and was generally regarded as a dependable promise. In recent years the form of a promise has remained, but a number of Europeans, and even some Americans, have come to wonder if it is only a half-empty threat. Perhaps it is, perhaps it is not; short of the actual test it is extremely difficult to predict with much confidence just what would happen. American action would depend heavily upon the nature and timing of the threat, the capabilities (local and nonlocal, nuclear and conventional) available to meet it, and the personalities of those making the decision. The United States has attempted to strengthen its position in a number of ways—by providing the military capability to respond flexibly to different kinds of hypothetical attacks; by trying to develop a multilateral nuclear deterrent for NATO; and by reaffirming in various ways its commitment to Europe's defense. Nevertheless a nuclear war over Europe would inevitably involve far more damage to the United States than it would have even a decade ago (almost certainly some tens of millions dead), and America's probable reaction does seem a good deal less predictable than it once was.

Some of our allies, notably France, have sought additional means of self-defense—means which inevitably include their own strategic nuclear weapons. If they can develop respectable deterrents their dependence on the United States will be lessened, as will the biopolarity of the system.

In other ways too bipolarity has weakened a little. Since 1945 a major goal of American foreign policy has been the unification of Western Europe, the creation of a state large enough and cohesive enough to defend its own interests and to serve as a powerful if sometimes slightly independent ally of the United States. To a significant degree this policy has succeeded, at least on the limited scale of "little Europe." "Little Europe," as contrasted with the entire Western European continent plus Britain, has come to mean the six states of the common market: France, Germany, Italy, and the Benelux countries. Integration has pushed farthest there, especially in economic affairs but also in matters of atomic energy and explicitly political affairs. These six countries have, among them, a population almost as large as America's and a G.N.P. which exceeds that of the Soviet Union. To the extent that they act as a unit in world politics they can approach the strength of a superpower.

Finally there is the division within the Communist bloc. The Chinese and Russians have split over a number of issues. They differ in their interpretation of Marxist ideology. The Chinese are resentful over Russian economic aid to neutralist regimes, which they feel should have been kept within the bloc—that is, it should have gone to China. They are angry because the Soviets provided so little help in building Chinese nuclear strength, and they even signed the test-ban treaty in an apparent effort to stifle Chinese efforts. They assess the risks of nuclear war as lower than the Russians seem to, and therefore advocate a more aggressive policy in trying to take over underdeveloped countries. And the Chinese have a millennia-old tradition, born in part of China's one-time cultural superiority, of disdain and even contempt for "barbarous" foreigners. Though the Russians may be fellow Communists, they also, to the Chinese, are barbarians.

These are hardly attitudes designed to maintain a close alliance, and as is abundantly clear the alliance has not in recent years been close. It is a rash man who would be certain that, in a major international crisis, the two great Communist powers would not actively support each other. Yet, as perhaps with NATO for somewhat different reasons, one cannot be sure of the opposite either. In any case the split has meant that China and Russia are competing with each other in important ways. They are Russian and Chinese wings to the Communist parties of many underdeveloped countries. These wings advocate rather different policies and sometimes conflict bitterly. China's economic development has been hindered by the withdrawal of Soviet aid. Both have been damaged by the reduction in commerce. In the six years from 1956 to 1962 trade with China dropped from 21 per cent of all Soviet foreign trade to only 5 per cent.

As we said, it is too early to know precisely the extent to which the bipolar world has become less sharply divided into two distinct segments. But in the following chapters we can examine some of the problems more closely, with an effort to be as precise as possible and to rely upon objective and carefully weighed evidence. Political scientists, to be scientific, must take care that the evidence they use is reliable, unbiased, and appropriate to the propositions they wish to investigate. While trying, in the pages to come, to describe the world as it is and was we shall try also to illustrate some techniques for description and for testing hypotheses. We will discuss the uses of these techniques in the context of some speculation about the over-all development of the international system. It will be impossible to explore all the problems we would have to look at to gain a full understanding of the system, but we can highlight and clarify some trends. Our interest in trends will provide a frame of reference within which to fit our specific explorations.

The subjects chosen for study were picked according to two criteria: they should be amenable to analysis by means of some of these objective techniques and, even more important, should be centrally related to possible major changes in the international system. Thus we focus on divisive and unifying forces within NATO—a key determinant of the degree of bipolarity in the system, on potential changes in the United Nations political process, and on the possible rise of a revolutionary have-not power.

CHAPTER 2

The Growth of Atlantic Institutions

International and Supranational Organizations

One of the most striking, and one of the most important, developments of the postwar world has been the growth of a wide variety of institutions linking various nations of the North Atlantic area (that is, Western Europe and North America). These institutions were created to fill specific needs for producing common or compatible policies among the nations of the area, and have been directed to a number of different problems and have involved different countries. In membership they have ranged from such small organizations as the Benelux (Belgium-Netherlands-Luxembourg) Customs Union to the 21-member Organization for Economic Co-operation and Development. Their functions have been variously economic, military, cultural, and political.

They also have differed greatly in the degree to which the member governments have delegated power to the new institutions. Some have been merely agencies for the co-ordination of national policies; others have involved a significant element of governmental authority above the nation-state members. We may distinguish between two kinds of institutions, both of which currently exist within the North Atlantic area. The distinction is concerned with the amount of independence reserved by the member states and is between an *international* (among nations) organization and a *supranational* (above nations) one.[1]

1. In a supranational organization decisions are taken by *majority vote* of the membership. The majority may be qualified (requiring perhaps two thirds or three fourths of the membership), but no single state has a veto, as in an international organization.
2. In a supranational organization a decision is *binding* on all members, including any who voted against the decision. In an international organization decisions merely have the status of recommendations.

[1] The following distinctions are adapted from Ernst Haas, *The Uniting of Europe* (Stanford: Stanford University Press, 1958), pp. 35–37.

3. In a supranational organization there is an *executive* with the authority to carry out decisions; an international organization is dependent upon the executive branches of its member governments.
4. In a supranational organization *persons* (both physical persons and legal persons like corporations) are directly subject to its authority; in an international organization the only members and subjects are states, which are the intermediaries in dealings with persons.
5. In a supranational organization the decision makers are *not instructed* by their local governments and are free to vote as their personal values and interests may dictate. In an international organization the decision makers are almost always instructed by their national governments.
6. In a supranational organization the institution itself may *expand its powers* in response to new conditions and demands; the powers of an international organization can be expanded only through the initiative of the member governments.
7. In a supranational organization *withdrawal* is extremely difficult, and the organization is usually intended to be permanent. Supranational organizations usually involve such major delegation of decision making from the member states that the whole fabric of the institution would be destroyed by the attempted withdrawal of a major member. An international organization, however, is governed by the law of treaties and the implicit assumption (*pacta sunt servanda, rebus sic stantibus*—agreements are to be kept, conditions remaining the same) that it is possible to withdraw from them.

With these definitions we have distinguished between two ideal types. Naturally many real-life institutions do not fit either of the two sets of definitions perfectly, and a number of the organizations in the North Atlantic area contain both international and supranational elements. But the use of these basic distinctions will give us some base line against which to judge the degree of institutional integration and delegation of authority in various organizations covering different numbers of nations. We now must look at the development of some of the major Atlantic institutions involving three or more nations since 1945.

Some Institutions

The Brussels Treaty Organization (1948). Members: Britain, France, and the three Benelux nations. This was primarily a military alliance, providing for an organization to co-ordinate the members' military efforts, and a consultative committee consisting of the foreign ministers that was to meet every three months. It was strictly an international, rather than a supranational, organization. The executive body of the organization was empowered only to make recommendations.

Organization for European Economic Co-operation (OEEC) (1948). Members: the 18 states of Western Europe, including all European countries outside the Soviet Bloc except Finland and Yugoslavia. (Spain, however, did not join until 1959.) The OEEC was set up to administer the European Recovery Program and to allocate American aid under the Marshall Plan, to co-ordinate investment, and to get European trade moving again. Decisions were taken by the Council, in which all member states had equal representation. The decisions were taken by majority vote and, though not binding on the whole group, did bind those states that approved them in the first place. The organization had a Secretariat, which undertook studies and inquiries for the Council. Also two executive agencies, the European Productivity Agency and the European Nuclear Energy Agency, were set up, responsible to the Council. The latter has undertaken a number of projects for the development of production and research facilities in Europe.

North Atlantic Treaty Organization (NATO) (1949). Members: The United States, Canada, Britain, France, West Germany, the Benelux countries, Italy, Denmark, Norway, Portugal, Greece, and Turkey. The foremost organ of NATO is the Council of ministers or heads of state, which meets three times a year. Decisions must be unanimous and carry the weight of recommendations only, but important bargaining and negotiation goes on. Under the Council is the Standing Group of the Military Committee, which is in permanent session in Washington and provides strategic direction and co-ordinated defense plans. It is composed of senior miliary officers whose decisions are, of course, subject to approval by their national political and military superiors. An international Staff/Secretariat, composed of nationals of all members and recruited as an international civil service, constantly surveys the military requirements of the allies, examines their economic conditions and resources, and reviews and criticizes their efforts and sets up targets for national recruitment, organization, and production. A unified command was set up with a Supreme Allied Commander (SACEUR), and below him various regional ground, sea, and air commanders, each leading forces contributed by more than one nation. Three types of military units were distinguished: those over which SACEUR had operational control of training and development, those merely earmarked for his control in time of war, and those that remained entirely under national command. NATO was most effective in the Central Europe Command, but even there it did not include all the various national forces actually stationed in the area, and particularly excluded some tactical air forces and all strategic nuclear weapons, owing primarily to American unwillingness to share information or control of nuclear weapons. The NATO commander's control was likely to be firm only in time of maneuvers, as indicated by a comment of the organization's first Secretary General that SACEUR might "deal direct with national authorities . . . to settle with them how the forces could be employed in peacetime." [2] Naval forces under Supreme Allied Command Atlantic were merely earmarked. British and French earmarked units were prepared and used for the assault on Suez in 1956 without the knowledge of SACEUR. And forces could always be withdrawn entirely from NATO control, as the French have done with important units.

NATO undoubtedly represents the most tightly integrated peacetime alliance among free nations in history. Nevertheless, it is clearly, especially in the light of nations' ability to withdraw their forces, an international rather than a supranational organization. Current differences over nuclear strategy, and both French and British efforts to maintain a deterrent force independent of the United States, suggest some of the basic strains within the alliance. It probably functioned more effectively in the 1950's than in recent years. In any case integration was never as close as between the United States and Britain during World War II—when both nations certainly retained their sovereignty.

Council of Europe (1949). Members: same as OEEC, but excluding Spain and Portugal and including Cyprus. It is concerned with a variety of political and cultural matters, and consists of a Committee of Ministers, most of whose decisions require a unanimous vote, and a Consultative Assembly. The Committee of Ministers usually consists of the foreign ministers of the various governments, and the Assembly of members of the national parliaments. In no sense is the executive responsible to the Assembly. The Assembly's purpose is to discuss and to arouse public sentiment in favor of unity; though it has the power of recommendation only, the degree to which the representatives sometimes divide along party (Socialist versus Christian Democrat) rather than national (French versus German) lines is striking.

[2] General Hastings Lionel Ismay, *NATO: The First Five Years* (Utrecht: Bosch, 1955), p. 72.

European Coal and Steel Community (ECSC) (1952). Members: France, West Germany, Italy, and Benelux. It was organized to provide a common market, without tariffs or other trade restrictions, in coal and iron products. One of the most ambitious of the Atlantic institutions, it has been one of the most successful. Though operating in the economic realm, it always has had explicit overtones of furthering the political unification of its members—one of its primary purposes was to intertwine the French and German economies so tightly that independent German military action would be impossible. The primary executive organ is the High Authority, composed of nine experts, uninstructed by their governments, who are empowered to act by majority vote rather than unanimity. Their powers include the right to levy taxes, to control prices, to channel investments, to raise loans and credits, to allocate coal and steel during periods of shortage, and to fix production levels during times of surplus. It is responsible to a Common Assembly, which can, by a two-thirds vote, force the High Authority to resign as a body. The Authority must also co-operate with a Council of Ministers (representatives of the member governments), who take decisions by majority vote. A Court of Justice rules on legal questions arising from the Community's actions. Though the Community's powers are limited in the sphere to which they apply, they are substantial, and it is clearly a supranational rather than an international organization. Its principal weakness in theory, which has not seriously hindered its operation, has been the absence of an administrative agency capable of enforcing its decisions; it has had to depend upon the co-operation of member governments in accepting and carrying out decisions to which they are legally bound.

Western European Union (WEU) (1955). Members: France, West Germany, Italy, Benelux, and Britain. This is primarily a military organization, set up in response to the failure of the European Defense Community to be ratified in the face of an obvious need for a German military contribution to Western defense. It is essentially an extension of the Brussels Treaty Organization, and includes a joint military command under NATO. It has an Assembly of Parliamentarians, a Consultative Council, and a small Secretariat over groups like the Agency for the Control of Armaments (primarily to see that Germany observes its treaty commitments not to produce certain kinds of weapons, especially nuclear ones), and the Standing Armaments Committee (to work for standardization and co-ordination of arms procurement). Formally it involves some delegation of sovereign powers, for some decisions of the group can be taken by a simple or two-thirds majority vote. The British, for example, committed themselves to maintain four divisions on the Continent of Europe, and to remove them they would have to obtain the approval of a majority of WEU's members. As early as 1957, however, Britain decided it would have to move some of its troops stationed in Germany back to the British Isles. Although they obtained the formal approval of WEU and so kept their treaty obligations, it was clear from their behavior that the British intended to withdraw those troops in any case, if necessary in defiance of a majority. WEU is not a supranational organization, and in fact has been rather moribund.

European Economic Community (EEC) (1958). Members: the "Six" of Continental Europe, who were members of the ECSC. This is the "Common Market," organized ostensibly for pursuing economic goals but also for furthering the political unity of the member states. It is directed not just to the removal of trade barriers, but to the development of a true common market involving common agricultural prices and subsidies, the harmonization of social welfare systems and wage policies, putting competition on an equal footing in all countries, a common transport policy, and the free movement of capital and labor across national boundaries. The individual states under these terms lose many of their most powerful tools for dealing with business cycle fluctuations; thus important powers are delegated to the various agencies of the EEC. It has an Assembly, which incorporates the Assembly that previously existed for the Coal and Steel Community. Like the ECSC Assembly, it can censure its Commission by a two-thirds vote. The Commission is the operating authority, with an executive differentiated into a number of agencies including the European Investment Bank, which makes loans to governments and private authorities for development within the Community. Major policies are initiated in the Council of Ministers, where increasingly decisions will be taken by a qualified majority vote. The element of majority vote, and the wide scope of the powers delegated to the Community, make this clearly a supranational organization of great significance. Its success is measured by the unanimously agreed shortening of the transition period, and by the high rate of economic growth achieved by its members—a rate unsurpassed by any other group of nations in the world.

European Atomic Energy Community (Euratom) (1958). Members: the Six. It was organized to further the civil exploitation of nuclear energy; it undertakes no activities in the military field, but it does not prevent its members from doing so. Its primary functions relate to the purchase and production of nuclear fuels; it supervises patents and the application of discoveries, promotes and co-ordinates investment, and operates a research center. It has a five-member Commission, responsible to the same Assembly as exists for EEC and ECSC. It too can be replaced by a two-thirds vote of censure. Although it clearly incorporates supranational elements, its powers are actually fairly narrowly circumscribed, and the French government in particular has given rather detailed instructions to its member of the Commission.

European Free Trade Association (EFTA) (1959). Members: Britain, Sweden, Norway, Denmark, Switzerland, Austria, and Portugal. Organized by the British as a direct response to the EEC, it was intended as a stopgap and a means of applying pressure to the negotiations for association with the EEC on terms less demanding than those accepted by the Six. Though there were to be no trade restrictions within the area, it involved no common external tariff, thus allowing the British to maintain their system of Commonwealth preference. Agricultural products were excluded from its provisions. Given its restricted functions there was no need for institutions with supranational powers; its Council operates on the rule of unanimity, though its decisions are binding. Even as a purely international organization it has foundered.

Organization for Economic Co-operation and Development (OECD) (1961). Members: all members of the former OEEC, plus the United States, Canada, and Japan. This is essentially an extension of the OEEC to include the other major industrial countries. It remains an international organization, with power of recommendation only, for promoting trade and economic development in the North Atlantic Area.

The Trend Toward Little Europe

Several elements emerge from this discussion: First, North Atlantic integration has proceeded on a broad front, encompassing a great range of political, economic, and military matters. This wide range is one of the movement's great strengths, because it has been able to affect and involve such a variety of individuals and public and private agencies. Some of the primarily economic institutions have been those where the highest degree of integration, the greatest element of supranationality, have been achieved. This applies to the

Coal and Steel Community, the Common Market, and Euratom, though not to OEEC and its successor OECD, and not to the Free Trade Association. Involving the next greatest element of delegation of sovereignty, at some substantial distance, are the military organizations, NATO and Western European Union. Still further behind is the most explicitly political institution, the Council of Europe. If one were to rank these organizations in terms of their *success,* the groupings would almost certainly be just the same.

Second, there seems to be a trend, not altogether unmixed but still discernible, toward increases in the element of supranationalism. The first institution with important supranational overtones was the ECSC, instituted in 1952. This was followed by Euratom and the Common Market in 1958. Although the latter two organizations look no more supranational than the first in terms of the kinds of powers they exercise, in the Common Market at least the powers apply to a much broader range of concerns.

Third, on the whole, supranationality—and perhaps success—is inversely related to the breadth of geographical coverage. The greatest surrender of national power, and the greatest success, has been achieved with organizations limited in their membership to the Six of Continental Europe. The broadest organizations, OEEC–OECD and NATO, tend to be those with the least delegation of authority to the central agencies. Much the same can be said for those institutions that, though they do not include the United States and Canada, have Britain as a member—Western European Union and, especially, the Council of Europe. The greatest failure has undoubtedly been that group which *failed* to include any of the central Six—the Free Trade Association.

By far the countries of the Six have been most willing to move in the direction of unification, at least among themselves. Not surprisingly the United States, though favoring unity for others, has not been ready to commit its power of independent action (except for some steps under NATO) with other nations divided from it by so much distance and historical tradition of separateness. More striking, perhaps, is the way this brief review highlights British isolation. The British government was never very enthusiastic about either OEEC or the Council of Europe, which it nevertheless joined. It made fairly frequent use of its veto rights in OEEC, and was largely responsible for the restrictions placed upon the powers of the Council of Europe Assembly when it was created. Britain refused to participate in the original negotiations for the Common Market, as it had declined an invitation to join the Coal and Steel Community six years earlier. In the first instance Harold Macmillan, then in opposition to the Labour Government, declared: "One thing is certain and we may as well face it. Our people will not hand over to any supranational Authority the right to close down our pits or our steelworks." [3] Britain's intention to limit her commitment to Europe was well illustrated by her decision, in 1957, to withdraw a division of troops from Germany. Even Winston Churchill, who in the late 1940's so eloquently advocated the creation of a United Europe, made it clear that by Europe he meant the Continent only. Thus Britain's belated attempt, in 1961, to seek membership in the Common Market marked a historic reversal—but a reversal for economic reasons, not because political unity with the Continent looked attractive.

Churchill spoke for many Britishers when he characterized his country's role as that of a link between America and Western Europe, part of a larger Atlantic community but maintaining its independence from either of the other major components. Britishers prized (probably more than did Americans) the "special relationship" to the United States that seemed to guarantee to their country particular influence over Western strategic and political decisions. Britishers also saw themselves as historically and by duty bound to the Commonwealth; any event that forced them to make a choice between the two would have to be decided in favor of the Commonwealth. The most serious specific issue in her negotiations with the Six (not excluding her desire to protect British agriculture) was the fact that entry into the Common Market would require her to abandon trade preferences with her Commonwealth partners, which in turn would result in a weakening of the political bonds.

But other elements also contributed to Britain's aloofness. For years she had acted as the "balancer" in Europe's balance of power system, protecting her own security by preventing any state from gaining predominance. To foster, or to participate in, an effort to end Continental divisions required a hard decision. Finally, Britishers were acutely aware of, and perhaps exaggerated, their political and cultural

[3] Quoted in U. W. Kitzinger, *The Politics and Economics of European Integration* (New York: Frederick A. Praeger, 1963), p. 11. On the institutional and political developments of this period also see Max Beloff, *New Dimensions in Foreign Policy* (New York: The Macmillan Company, 1961), and George Lichtheim, *The New Europe: Today—and Tomorrow* (New York: Burns and MacCachern, 1963).

differences from the major states across the Channel. Unlike Britain, the Six share the Roman law tradition, are predominantly Roman Catholic, and the big countries have a disturbing heritage of political instability. The British Labour Party is in some ways even more suspicious of Europe than are the Conservatives—in part because winning elections with a Socialist majority seems more probable in England alone than it does in a wider Europe with its strong Liberal, Christian Democratic, and, in France and Italy, even Communist parties.

Just the same, not all of the separation between Britain and the Continent can be blamed on the British. France has historically regarded England as her rival, hardly less so than Germany. General De Gaulle also retained from his wartime experiences strong suspicions of the Anglo-Saxon powers and the sincerity of Britain's belated profession of attachment to Europe. By the 1950's Frenchmen, especially De Gaulle, had come to see that West Germany (properly weakened by the loss of her Eastern territories) could serve as a means of increasing French power. France had the diplomatic skills, and still the respectability, to hold a pre-eminent role in political decisions on the Continent. Germany, furthermore, was prepared to make important concessions to French interests. During his long chancellorship Konrad Adenauer sought to knit Germany into Europe as a means of protecting Germans from the worst in themselves. In addition the West German government felt the need of forceful diplomatic support on Berlin, and the British all too often seemed ready to temporize and bargain. Thus strong forces operated to maintain the cleavage between the British Isles and the Continent, forces that creative statesmen could try to control but to which they might also have to accommodate themselves.

What Is a Community?

At this point we must begin to look in a different way at the forces working for and against the integration of the Atlantic community and its separate regions. We will develop this effort further in the following chapter, but here we must make some additional basic distinctions and set the growth in institutions within a wider framework. Often we speak of the North Atlantic area as a "community." What do we mean? Certainly we do not mean just a geographical area or a military alliance. Usually we imply some or all of the following:

1. The people of the area share a *common culture and historical tradition,* a Christian culture (some would say post-Christian) and the heritage of Western Civilization. There are different subcultures within the area (Italy is surely different from Britain), and there are other countries, not in the North Atlantic area, that also share this culture to some degree (for example, Latin America, Eastern Europe). Nevertheless, in a vague sense we still think of the North Atlantic countries as somehow similar, and distinct from the rest of the world. In other words, the people of these countries share certain common values—or where the values are not *common,* on the whole they are *compatible.* That is, though they may not agree, at least the disagreement does not result in conflict. In some important respects the values of Catholics and Protestants, for example, are not identical, but they are sufficiently compatible that they usually do not lead to political conflict.

2. The people share a *sense* of homogeneity, a *sense* of shared values and interests and of a common identity. Thus the common culture must be felt subjectively, rather than simply something observed by an outside spectator. In a way this says that the *important* values are believed to be common or compatible. The sense of a common identity becomes a test of agreement or compatibility of important values.

3. A community not only may share common interests, it may have a sense of common interests *as opposed to those outside* the community. Thus to some extent the peoples of the North Atlantic may feel a threat to their way of life, to their political, economic, and social institutions, and to their high standard of living from either or both of two sources: the Communist Bloc and the underdeveloped world. It is well, however, not to overemphasize this element of external pressure. One can imagine a *world community* that did not depend for its cohesion on a threat from outer space.

4. The people share an expectation of the *peaceful settlement of disputes.* Inevitably conflict will arise within the community, but the people do not expect it to erupt into large-scale violence, but to be settled through agreed-upon channels. In general the countries of the North Atlantic area no longer consider war among themselves to be at all likely, though there are exceptions—Greece and Turkey over Cyprus perhaps the most important.

Now it is essential to note that the existence of a community is a *relative* matter. It is possible to have more or less of it over time, and we can say that some countries within the North Atlantic area share a higher degree of community than do all the countries together. Thus it is relative over time and between areas, and it implies a *relationship.* One cannot talk about a community without specifying which peoples or areas are contained in it and which ones (if any) are not.

Finally, community implies a *disposition* that we may call responsiveness, the readiness to respond favorably to a request from another member of the community. We can distinguish between responsiveness and the response to an individual request or demand. Merely because the level of community is low does not mean that a particular problem will be poorly handled. The chances are that it will not be met adequately, but in the short term one problem may be expedited and another botched. Responsiveness is the *probability* that the demands of one party will be met. *Responsiveness* is a general term giving us, in the specific case, a probability statement.

Capabilities for responsiveness include specific capabilities for *attention, communication,* and *mutual identification* within the community. Attention to other individuals and countries must be coupled with communication with them to perceive their vital interests and to transmit those perceptions to the points in the first country's decision-making centers, where they will be given quick and adequate treament. The facilities for attention and communication within a community of nations are formal international and supranational institutions, informal practices, and habits and memories of attention. (These may in turn depend upon the physical channels, such as telegraph cables, but it is the use made of these channels, not their physical existence, to which we refer.) An additional factor is covered by a class of attitudes, of self-images and mutual interests and mutual identification, loyalties, trust, and willingness to treat each other's requests sympathetically. This set of attitudes, which we will refer to simply as "mutual identification," cannot exist without the other two factors, but communication and attention need not, by themselves, produce mutual identification.

Without these capabilities co-operative international relations, or alliances, or the integration of several countries into a larger unit like a United States of Europe, are all exposed to serious risks. The amount of risk involved depends at any particular time on the *burdens* that correspond to the capabilities, on the demands made upon the capabilities for responsiveness. Demands may come both from outside a particular community and from within it, but in talking about community we will address ourselves to demands from within. These need not, of course, be "demands" in the sense of formal communications from one government to another. They include informal requests, pleas made by private individuals or agencies either to a government or to other private individuals, and merely "situations" that need attention, whether or not an explicit request is ever made. When the American government sends emergency disaster aid to an earthquake-stricken country it is demonstrating its capabilities for responsiveness even though it might not have been specifically asked for assistance.

Now an alliance may be maintained for a long time, or a nation may remain united for a long time, even if its capabilities for responsiveness are not especially high. It may do so either because of external pressures that tend to reinforce unity, such as the Soviet threat did for NATO during the 1950's; because of capabilities for hierarchical control, as in the Soviet Bloc; or because the burdens, or internal strains, are not severe. But if the strains become serious, either capabilities must likewise be strengthened or major failures of responsiveness become probable. As long as American willingness to undertake massive retaliation in response to an attack on Western Europe was not challenged by substantial Soviet power to strike the United States in return, NATO could manage with lower capabilities for mutual responsiveness among its members than later became necessary.

Actual responsiveness, then, depends upon some combination of two influences—attention to requests and willingness to consider them favorably. An unfavorable response may result either from inattention—a failure to be aware that a request was made—or from a deliberate decision not to meet a demand. Or the reverse: a favorable response may either be deliberate or it can occur "accidentally" despite a failure of attention, as domestic or other international pressures result in a response that meets the other party's needs even though no request was received. In practice, of course, it is very hard to identify the separate effects of attention and willingness to respond favorably—and most decisions undoubtedly involve both—but the distinction should nevertheless be clear.

Institutions as Capabilities

In the next chapter we shall discuss some influences that can be measured fairly precisely but that are sometimes slighted in studies of international integration. But in the context of this chapter we must return to a general evaluation of international and supranational institutions as capabilities. Political structures that embrace the governments concerned serve both as indicators of the existence of community and as important contributors to it. A high level of responsiveness may perhaps exist without institutions (before World War II there were few formal bonds between the United States and Canada), but they are usually necessary if there are many objects of mutual concern requiring common or compatible policies. Institutions provide important capabilities for attention and communication. An institution can be described as essentially a set of channels for processing information, transmitting communications, and solving problems. NATO is composed of a number of structures—the North Atlantic Council, the Military Committee, the Standing Group, and the Staff/Secretariat, among others—whose function is to provide strategic direction and co-ordinated defense plans. These represent permanent means for discussing military problems and working out solutions to mutual difficulties. Without these institutional channels it would be immensely harder for the NATO countries to co-ordinate their defense, reduce frictions, and avoid duplication even to the extent that they are able to do so now. Furthermore, a number of institutions imply not just channels for communication, negotiation, and discussion, but agreed-upon agencies for delegating responsibility and reaching binding decisions. In the Council of Ministers of the European Common Market, for instance, no one state has a veto power over actions of the Council. By giving a qualified majority the power to act, binding all members, this institution gives the members of the Common Market important capabilities for acting in a responsive manner toward each other and for advancing their mutual interests.

We must always remember, however, that no institution—and especially a supranational organization—is desirable merely for its own sake. Such an institution, entered into by free peoples, is supposed to increase mutual responsiveness and promote the common interest of its members. A structure, whether international or supranational, is meant to provide a capability for rapid and effective action in the pursuit of individual and common goals. But it may also bring burdens. It may result in a situation where too many capabilities are focused on the higher level with proportionately too few left on the level of the individual nation. Particular groups within some of the member countries may feel that their interests are being neglected at the expense of those outside the nations. German farmers, for instance, might decide that the Common Market was to blame for their economic difficulties, and their wrath could put serious strain both on the Common Market as a whole and on Germany itself. Delegation of power to a higher and wider level may produce conflicts that could otherwise have been prevented. The existence of a common government with the power to execute decisions against the will of some members may result in very severe stress and a sense of coercion.

Some of the bloodiest and most bitter wars have been between areas that were under a common government but whose capabilities for responsiveness were not equal to the burdens upon the system. No American should forget the Civil War in this context, and few Irishmen are likely to forget the century-long struggle for independence from English rule.

The experience of the past two decades, however, suggests that within the North Atlantic area the structures, international or in some cases supranational, have usually brought more capabilities than burdens, and that it will not be seriously inaccurate to treat the existence of structures as indicators of particularly important and politically relevant capabilities for responsiveness. At the same time we shall remember that a common government in the North Atlantic area is not necessarily to be desired. We may be much more interested in seeing that common, or at least compatible, policies are followed by the various nations in the area. The pursuit of an Atlantic, or of a European, government is a much more ambitious, and possibly a much less important, goal than is minimizing the kind of rivalry and incompatibility that has been fairly common between France and the Anglo-Saxon powers in recent years.

CHAPTER 3

Trends Within the North Atlantic Community

Trade and Politics

In the last chapter we looked at the growth of institutions and discussed, in a very general and abstract way, a kind of scheme for analyzing some basic factors underlying the relations among different countries. But we need some concrete methods of measuring whether capabilities, other than institutions, are high or low. In this chapter we shall examine certain kinds of facilities or transactions and trace trends in their growth or decline. Thus we shall be looking at *indicators* of capabilities, specific kinds of facilities that are measurable and that, taken together, may give us an idea of the over-all situation.

At one time it was easy, among people interested in international politics, to start a spirited argument over whether "trade follows the flag" or just the opposite, "the flag follows trade." Actually both are true in different cases. Trade is more than just an economic relationship. It tends quite strongly to mirror political and social community. In the modern world there are many possible suppliers for most goods. But few markets are perfectly competitive, because the products of two sellers are seldom identical. Customs, habits, traditions, notions about the goods or the seller, all differentiate two seemingly identical products. A seller who speaks the language and understands the attitudes of his customers has a great advantage over one who does not. Past habits can affect current prices through credit terms. Goods coming across a previously established trade route can be shipped more cheaply than those coming across a route that has not yet developed much traffic. Thus trade is one indicator of pre-existing political and cultural integration.

Trade also plays a major role as a *capability* for responsiveness, as a force making closer political ties possible. A person engaged in international commerce is exposed to a wide variety of information and ideas that would otherwise never reach him; he must listen to viewpoints that he would otherwise never hear. Trade can be a means by which the needs of one country are made known to another. An exporter is likely to have a general interest in the well-being of his market, an interest that transcends the marketing conditions, narrowly defined, for his product. But it is essential to understand that the effect is not limited to economic interests; an exporter may become attuned to the needs of the importing country over a great range of non-economic matters. In his study of France's decision to reject the European Defense Community in 1954, Daniel Lerner found that businessmen who engaged in no export trade were three times more likely to oppose EDC and favor maintenance of a French national army than were businessmen whose firms exported over half their production. In only a very few cases could any of these industrialists be said to have a direct "economic interest" in the decision.[1]

In addition, economic interests tend to bias decisions; an individual may act to further his financial interests. From the other side, persons who are predisposed to a particular decision will try to mobilize available economic interest groups for the support of that decision. That is, economic interests may "determine" political decisions, or they may merely be used to support those decisions. The question of "priority" is here irrelevant; we are concerned with interdependence, not determination.

Subject to the qualifications mentioned below, it can be argued that every political interest group has a power base, or power potential, that is roughly proportional to the share of the national income its members control. As the group's share in the national income rises, we should expect its *potential* power to increase. Not only would the group become more important as a means of communication between nations, but it would have more direct influence over political decision making.

To repeat, economic strength does not *determine* political decisions, but like ideology, noneconomic interest groups, and parties, it does constitute an important factor. Interest groups have numerous ways to influence a political figure. They can contribute to his campaign funds and provide facilities he needs for election. They can stimulate the flow of approval, demands, or criticism from his constituency.

[1] Daniel Lerner, "French Business Leaders Look at EDC," *Public Opinion Quarterly*, XX, **1** (1956), p. 220. In a study of British and American legislators (Senators and Members of Parliament) I similarly found a high correlation between trade contacts and responsiveness to the other country. See Bruce M. Russett, *Community and Contention: Britain and America in the Twentieth Century* (Cambridge, Mass.: Massachusetts Institute of Technology Press, 1963), Ch. 9.

A legislator with a limited staff and little time for research may be greatly in need of information on the effects of various events and proposals; an interest group can often supply the data. It may also provide him with legal briefs, or if an amendment to a pending bill seems necessary, it can even provide the amendment all properly drafted. If a legislator is accustomed to relying on an interest group for information, the group has a powerful weapon in the threat of withdrawing its advice and assistance. A public campaign may mold popular opinion or at least mold the legislator's image of that opinion.

But of course the relative size of an interest group's economic base is not the only factor influencing its success. In the words of a classic study, "equal stakes do not produce equal pressures."[2] Others that matter include the group's capacity for organization, its previous experience, the degree to which it is concentrated in a few constituencies, and its nearness to the legislation at issue. Because they are concentrated in a few constituencies, importers, who have as much stake in tariff legislation as domestic producers, sometimes have trouble making their pressure effective on a wide variety of legislators. Yet even though the effectiveness of two different interest groups at the same time need not be proportional to the size of their economic bases, we would expect *changes* in size to be correlated, in the long run, with changes in effectiveness. A group with an increasing economic base would, we should expect, have rising influence over a long span, even though the lag might be substantial. And as previously indicated, commerce provides a means of communication, and one participating in it is likely to revise his attitudes on many matters which do not immediately affect his self-interest. We would expect a correlation between changes in the size of the interest affected and changes in its effectiveness as an instrument of international communication promoting responsiveness.

Now to say that trade can become an important capability for responsiveness does not mean that it is enough by itself to produce a high level of responsiveness. An increase in East-West trade (as well as cultural exchange) is often advocated as a major way of reducing Soviet-American tensions. But the differences of ideology and interest that separate the two great powers may be so great that even a fairly large rise in East-West trade would not have a noticeable impact. Also, trade, like most other transactions, *can* actually bring serious ill will. Financial crises and debt defaults can embitter the relations of two countries. If two countries are highly interdependent

[2] E. E. Schattschneider, *Politics, Pressures, and the Tariff* (Englewood Cliffs, N.J.: Prentice-Hall, 1935), p. 135.

and one of them suffers from severe economic instability, the other is almost certain to share the instability. Depression spreads from its origin by cutting other countries' exports. Irritation may also stem from a circumstance where one nation is the world's major exporter of a particular commodity. Put crudely, the importing state may feel exploited if the supply is controlled by a monopoly or oligopoly. Even government price supports or production controls, though adopted merely to maintain the income of one's own producers rather than directly to exploit the buyers, may nevertheless arouse hard feelings. For whatever reasons, the former high level of Cuban-American trade, in which some Cubans felt exploited, almost certainly contributed to support for Castro's anti-Americanism.

Thus one must be careful to avoid a crude or simple view of the interrelationship between trade and political relations, but they are related nonetheless. Within the North Atlantic area the deleterious effects of trade are likely to be minimized, and it seems safe to regard it, on balance, as providing a capability for responsiveness. We may believe that a high level in trade provides substantial capabilities.

Table 3.1 **Exports to Various Countries per Thousand Dollars of Importing Country's G.N.P.**

	To France	*To West Germany*	*To Britain*	*To United States*
From France				
1938	—	1.3	3.4	.6
1952	—	7.0	5.5	.5
1963	—	15.8	5.1	.7
From West Germany				
1938	4.3	—	5.0	.7
1952	7.6	—	5.0	.7
1963	23.0	—	7.0	1.9
From Britain				
1938	5.7	3.3	—	1.7
1952	4.8	5.5	—	1.4
1963	7.2	7.1	—	1.7
From United States				
1938	6.7	2.6	17.4	—
1952	8.9	13.7	15.2	—
1963	9.6	12.8	14.6	—

SOURCES:

1938 and 1952: U.N., Statistical Papers, Series T, Vol. IV, No. 1/2, *Direction of International Trade* (New York: United Nations, 1954).

1963: OECD, Statistical Bulletins, Series A, *Foreign Trade: Overall Trade by Countries,* March 1964.

1938 data apply to all of Germany.

Table 3.1 shows trends in trade among the major Atlantic states since 1938. We show exports from each to each, expressed as a proportion of the importing country's G.N.P. Giving the volume of trade as a proportion of G.N.P. permits us to compare the potential political effects of trade in different instances, and the use of several separate points in time allows us to examine trends.

In general we find an increase, sometimes modest, sometimes very striking, in NATO trade in recent years. The highest proportions, all in 1963, are Germany to France and France to Germany. Notice, then, the great amount of commercial interchange between the two great nations of the Common Market. We would, of course, expect that the Common Market, with its avowed purpose of stimulating trade among its members, would have such an effect, but the volume is nevertheless striking. The achievement is all the more impressive when we look at trends. Franco-German trade was very moderate in 1938, lower than the corresponding trade of either with Britain. Thus the proportionate growth—a tenfold increase from France to Germany—is the largest in the table.

Britain's commercial relations with these Common Market countries, both as an exporter and an importer, have never been very close. The proportions are fairly low, and they show no important increases. Britain's closest trade ties are now, as before, with the United States and with the Commonwealth. The United States shows a great trade with West Germany, and a significant commerce with France, but its trade with France is clearly well below that with Germany or Britain. American exports to and imports from Britain have not increased (as a proportion of G.N.P.) since 1938. America's imports from none of the NATO countries look very impressive, however, because of the relatively minor role that foreign trade plays in the American economy.

What we find, in sum, is a striking trade, both in its current volume and its rate of growth, between France and the German Federal Republic. This powerfully confirms our previous indications of a Paris-Bonn axis which is playing an ever-growing role in world affairs. This same set of indicators identifies the relative isolation of Great Britain from the Continent. Economic ties between the United States and the Continental powers are substantial, but less than those prevailing between the two Continental powers, and their growth has been less rapid. German-American trade is greater, and growing faster, than is trade between France and the United States. This tends to confirm the intuitive judgment that the set of political ties between Bonn and Washingon is closer than those between Paris and Washington.

Elites and Attentive Public

There are other kinds of attention and communication facilities we can look at to confirm or modify the conclusions suggested by trade patterns. We must pay special heed to communications between members of a certain stratum, the "elite." Though all citizens in a democracy have some influence over decision making, if only in the negative way of failing to vote, influence is not distributed evenly. Properly we should speak of "elites" rather than use the term only in the singular. There is a business elite, a military elite, a communications elite, a political elite or elites, and others. A member of one of these elites may be able to exert particular influence over one type of decision but not over others. There is no need to imply that members of a particular elite, whether by implicit or explicit agreement, operate substantially as a unit or "power elite," or that they make all the politically relevant decisions of a society. But a position of influence in certain areas of activity clearly gives an individual some bases of influence to transfer more or less successfully to other areas. A man with wealth often has some formal role in political decision making. If not, he may be intimate with the powerful. Skills important in his commercial activities may also be useful in the political arena. Or his wealth may enable him to hire the services of the skillful. His influence, whether potential or actual, is limited, but he undoubtedly has some advantages not available to those who lack his resources.

It is very difficult to study only communications among the elites of various nations, but if we expand our interests to include the so-called attentive public, our task becomes easier and still deals with important influences on policy making. This attentive public is that portion of the population, probably about 10 to 15 per cent, that is interested in foreign affairs and is reasonably well informed about them. People in this stratum discuss policy alternatives, and the political elites must compete for their approval.

A major facility for communication and attention between elites, and members of the attentive public, in different countries is personal contact and travel. We shall look both at the flow of tourists within the North Atlantic area and at the pattern of student exchanges. Not all tourists are members of any elite, of course, but most of them do belong to the attentive public—to a large degree their travel abroad is itself proof of an interest in foreign affairs. Students are not members of the elite either, but again they usually may properly be included in the attentive public. And many of them will, in their later careers, become influential in government and the corporate world. Former Rhodes scholars, for instance, find their experience an open sesame to many doors, and many of the most powerful figures in recent American government—Secretary of State Rusk, Senator Fulbright, Budget Director Gordon, and the late President Kennedy, to name a few—were influenced in important ways by their early years as students in Great Britain. There may be a substantial lag between student days and days at the pinnacle of public affairs, but the influence is often felt eventually. It is through this kind of contact that a common culture, and a sense of common culture, may develop.

As with trade, personal contact does not always increase capabilities for responsiveness. There is an old saying that familiarity breeds contempt. Close contact may only emphasize differences and show people what there is to dislike in each other. A fairly high level of contact between Frenchmen and Germans in the late nineteenth century may have had this effect. Tourists may not make good ambassadors—some observers might contend that they are on the average more obnoxious and less perceptive than their stay-at-home countrymen. Their impressions may be shallow, and the pleasant associations of their trips may be overwhelmed by primitive European plumbing or twentieth-century American commercialism. Many a voyager has left his country ready to like a foreign land and returned only too glad to have the experience behind him. An African student in Chicago (or in Moscow) may, as a result of racial discrimination, go home a violent anti-American (or anti-Communist).

An obvious factor in evaluating the effect of personal contact is the amount and kind of difference in the cultures involved, and another is certainly the personalities of those involved. But on the whole, contact results in a degree of sympathy or affection for the other culture or nation, or if not affection, at least understanding for some of the basic concerns and needs of its people.[3] Or if we cannot say even that much, we can conclude that *without* substantial personal contact two nations whose fates are closely intertwined, and who must frequently act upon each other at the governmental level, are very unlikely to be very responsive to each other's needs. That is, contact alone may not produce responsiveness, but it is difficult to have sustained responsiveness, without it. This is surely true of the nations which make up

[3] For some indications, if not positive proof, that this is true, see Russett, *op. cit.*, and the references there.

NATO, and in addition it would seem that their cultures are sufficiently similar, especially by comparison with those of Asia, Africa, and the Communist world, that contact tends to promote understanding. Thus trends in tourism and in student exchange will give us crude but useful indicators of a basic kind of cement underlying their political relations.

First we can look at student exchange. As with trade, it is important that we have not only the absolute number of students from and to each country but some indication of their relative importance. So this time we weight the student exchange by expressing it as students per 100,000 persons in the country of origin, on the assumption that the greater the relative number of students, the greater potential effect they may have. Table 3.2 gives the information. Unfortunately we have data only since the early 1950's, not going back to the prewar years.

Table 3.2 **Students from Various Countries per 100,000 Persons in Sending Country**

	From France	*From West Germany*	*From Britain*	*From United States*
In France				
1952	—	1.1	1.4	.6
1960	—	2.6	1.6	.6
In West Germany				
1952	.2	—	.3	.2
1959	.8	—	.5	.8
In Britain				
1952	.2	.3	—	.4
1961	.1	.4	—	.6
In United States				
1952	1.6	2.7	2.1	—
1961	1.3	1.6	2.1	—

SOURCE:
UNESCO, *Study Abroad, 1955* (Paris, 1954) and *1963* (Paris, 1962).

For recent years, the greatest movement is from West Germany to France. This exactly parallels our trade figures. The increase—more than double since 1952—is also impressive. The number of French students in Germany has also grown rapidly—a fourfold increase—but the absolute level is not nearly so great. The standing of German educational institutions was severely damaged by World War II, and the country has still not fully recovered its position as a leading center for educating students from abroad. (Also, unlike French and English, German is the native tongue for few people outside Germany, so a language barrier often inhibits foreign students from going to German universities.) France and the United States are the greatest magnets for attracting foreign students, but not too much vis-à-vis each other. Few Americans go to French universities, and vice versa; few, at least, relative to the influx from the other major NATO countries. The strength of the German-American tie is again attested to by the growing number of American students who go to the Federal Republic, though the number of Germans in American universities has actually declined since 1952. Both these events may reflect German recovery from the war. And finally, note again the seeming isolation of Great Britain, which does not receive substantial proportions of foreign students from any of the NATO countries, and especially from the Continent. Britain does send a fair-sized delegation to French universities, but not to German ones, and the Franco-British traffic is all one way. So we confirm most of our impressions from trade patterns—close ties, growing closer, between the two Continental powers, the isolation of Britain, and the intermediate position of the United States, a position that shows closer ties with Britain and Germany than with France.

For a further test we can examine trends in international tourism. Table 3.3 gives these data, again weighted to take account of the population of the sending country.

Table 3.3 Tourists from Various Countries per 1000 Persons in Sending Country

	From France	*From West Germany*	*From Britain*	*From United States*
In France				
1952	—	3	10	2
1962	—	15	14	4
In West Germany				
1952	4	—	4	2
1962	11	—	10	4
In Britain				
1952	2	1	—	1
1962	5	4	—	2
In United States				
1952	1	1	2	—
1962	1	1	2	—

SOURCES:

Tourists in U.S., 1952: U.N., *Statistical Yearbook, 1954* (New York: United Nations, 1955), p. 323.

All others: OEEC, *Tourism in Europe, 1953* (Paris, 1955), and OECD, *Tourism in Member Countries, 1963* (Paris, 1963).

This strengthens some of the conclusions suggested by the earlier tables but requires us to modify others. As in each of the first two instances, the highest relative volume of traffic is from Germany to France, with Germany sending 15 tourists per 1000 of population (1.5 per cent of all Germans) in 1962. The France-to-Germany traffic is also very high, at 11 per 1000 in the same year. But even higher (14) is British travel to France, and British tourism in Germany falls only a little short of that level (10). Germany and France again appear very close, especially in view of the marked increase in mutual tourism since as recently as 1952. Especially notable is the fivefold increase in Germans' travel to the land of their historic enemy in the west. But we find little evidence for British separateness from Europe, at least when we look at the habits of British travelers, who have traditionally spent their holidays on the Continent and show no signs of changing their habits; on the contrary, those habits are becoming more ingrained. French and German travel to Britain, however, is not so substantial when compared with that between themselves. Yet in this table the really isolated country is the United States, which tends neither to send nor to receive as many tourists. The reason is surely the nearly 4000-mile distance that even in this jet age separates America's east coast from Europe. Not only Europeans but many Americans too still find a transatlantic vacation expensive and beyond their means. The effect of this distance is to keep fairly weak a bond that might serve in useful ways to reconcile American and European attitudes.

Mass Communication

Elite attitudes are highly influential, but in no country, and certainly in no democracy, can mass perspectives be entirely ignored. "Elite" and "mass" are merely terms to designate groups at the extremes of a continuum, and we must look at the whole spectrum. Non-elite members of the populace may not be important in *initiating* policy; they may not even, in many circumstances, be important in molding or vetoing it. But mass opinion does set certain bounds beyond which decision makers may not go. Candidates for public office seldom dare to adopt obviously unpopular positions, and they usually tailor their policy recommendations to what they expect will meet with popular approval. In these negative and passive ways mass opinion does play a vital role in policy formation. And in the act of voting even many apathetic members of the populace take direct action in influencing decisions by determining who shall occupy the formal policy-making positions.

So we also need a measure of international contact between ordinary people. One indicator might be the amount of attention given to other countries' affairs in newspapers and magazines; another might be figures on the showings of foreign-made motion pictures; yet another might be data on international migration. All this information, however, is very hard to obtain for any substantial number of countries over any useful period of time—either (as for newspaper attention) it would require a major research project, or (as with migration) the records kept by governments are not adequate to give reliable, comparable information. But one good set of data does exist, and that is for the volume of mail—letters, to be precise—exchanged among various countries. This can give us some idea of the amount of international contact between people who are not in immediate personal contact through travel. Letters of course can be written for an infinite variety of reasons, some of no political import, some far from trivial, but we are speaking in general, of probabilities, and on the whole trends in mail can provide a reasonable index. Table 3.4 shows the number of letters sent, per person in the receiving country,

Table 3.4 **Letters to Various Countries per Person in Receiving Country**

	To France	*To West Germany*	*To Britain*	*To United States*
From France				
1937	—	.09	.35	.05
1952	—	.22	.23	.11
1961	—	.50	.40	.09
From West Germany				
1937	.13	—	.15	.05
1952	.19	—	.17	.10
1961	.57	—	.34	.18
From Britain				
1937	.30	.12	—	.13
1952	.20	.14	—	.21
1961	.30	.28	—	.21
From United States				
1932	.13	.12	.42	—
1952	.31	.37	.65	—
1961	.40	.54	.84	—

SOURCES:

Letters from U.S.: Communication from U.S. Post Office Department.

All others: Union Postale Universelle, *Statistiques des Expeditions dans le Service Postal International, 1937* (Berne, 1939); *1952* (Berne, 1954); and *1961* (Berne, 1963). The figures for 1937 are for all of Germany.

between each of the same four nations. As with trade, in this table we are again able to find data for the prewar period, and so examine trends over a full 25-year span.

Unlike all the earlier tables, here we find the greatest traffic to be from the United States to Europe, especially to Great Britain. This partly reflects America's size and wealth (the latter making postage a relatively insignificant item of expenditure). But except for the America-to-Britain traffic, the highest figures apply, as usual, between Germany and France, and, again as usual, especially from Germany westward. British-French and British-German mail is relatively moderate despite the fact that, especially in the British-French case, it started from a reasonably high level in 1937. British-French mail, in fact, shows a remarkably small increase, and not at all from Britain to France, over the whole period. French-German contact, however, shows a four- or five-fold rise. Finally, note that American contact with France is notably slighter than with either of the other two countries and shows the smallest increase. Thus on the whole we confirm our findings of ever-closer relations between the two major Continental states, Britain in a fairly isolated position, and the United States closest to Britain and farthest from France.

We will not get involved in the question of whether the chicken precedes the egg; in this case the degree to which a high level of trade, or travel, or mail flow *causes* responsiveness and the degree to which it merely *indicates* a pre-existing level of responsiveness. In our discussion so far we have emphasized the causal aspect, because we can be reasonably sure it does have this effect. But attention and communication, as measured by the particular indices, also indicate a responsiveness that was there already. Commercial transactions, for example, usually depend upon a certain degree of pre-existing understanding, and the transactions and the responsiveness may well reinforce each other. Two people in love may reinforce their love by behaving affectionately toward each other, or hate may beget mutual hatred, in such a way that it becomes virtually impossible to disentangle cause and effect. This kind of situation is often described as having "feedback." But we do not have to decide here the degree to which our indices of mail or travel produce capabilities for responsiveness and the degree to which they are produced by such capabilities—all we need to know is that they do indicate the existence of capabilities for responsiveness.

In seeking data on several different indices we should emphasize that no single index is fully satisfactory as a measure of the underlying influences we wish to know about. Different people are exposed to different means of communication; the various media have different effects on their viewers. Special influences, like trade restrictions, may distort the picture given by one index without affecting others. Thus it is essential to have several different measures, and to be very cautious in the conclusions we draw unless they are supported by similar trends in several different indices. This method is congenial for another reason—the state of our factual and theoretical understanding of international integration is not so good that we can isolate any one of these factors as being a great deal more influential than another. We cannot say with any certainty which is more important—this applies both as regards our basic variables, attention, communication, and mutual identification, and as regards the numerous alternative indices that might be available to measure them. What does in fact seem to be the case is that a high level of responsiveness depends upon a high level of all three variables, and favorable measurements on a number of indices. Attention, communication, and mutual identification must, if they are to bear heavy strains, be high over a wide variety of experiences with a wide variety of people. So for another reason we can speak with confidence about over-all international integration only when we have looked at many influences.

But our conclusions are quite consistent and allow us to make some fairly firm statements. One of the most important and perhaps least widely appreciated political developments of the past decades has been the Franco-German rapprochement. These two countries now seem closer together than ever before in their conflict-marred histories. The possibility of a permanent end to war and preparations for war between these two powers cannot be other than gratifying. Still, without tempering our gratitude, we must nevertheless recognize the new and not entirely welcome aspects of this development. One is indeed the relative isolation of Great Britain from the other states of Western Europe and, to a lesser degree, the clear failure of American-European integration to keep pace with what has been going on within the bounds of the Continent. Perhaps some eventual growing apart of Europe and America was inevitable; possibly not. In any event the emergence of a European power as an independent force becomes much more understandable in the light of our data, as is the determination of many Europeans to show their independence both of the United States and of Britain (who they feel has acted insufficiently "European"), and their internal cohesion. The process may or may not culminate in further formal, institutional unity among the Six, but we are unlikely to see much less co-ordination of the members' foreign policies, and in some real sense another major power is emerging. Whether or not it can retain its unity in the face of the internal differences of interest that will undoubtedly occur is uncertain, but important changes have been occurring.

In assessing these developments it is well to remember two things. First, French-American conflicts, especially over military questions, are not purely the consequence of the policies pursued by particular individuals, specifically Charles de Gaulle. The General's personality, special attitudes toward Anglo-Saxons, and sometimes grandiose ambitions for France of course aggravate matters, but to a very large degree he reflects, but does not create, a distance between France and the United States that precedes his political dominance and has been in the making for some time. Basic patterns of culture, economics, and politics are at work underneath the everyday clashes and agreements between heads of state. Second, let us recall that in no minor way the burying of the Franco-German hatchet, and the new independence of a united Europe that is its result, was a deliberate aim of American foreign policy after the Second World War. The Marshall Plan was conceived as a means to build a Europe once more able to stand on its own, and it has succeeded in important ways. Surely American policymakers did not foresee the precise frictions, either in kind or extent, that would arise from Europe's renewed vigor. But certainly we all would prefer the present differences to a world where Europe was weak, divided, and totally dependent upon American defense against Communist aggression. There is yet a third kind of world, however, that we might prefer to either of these—a more closely integrated Atlantic Community. Unfortunately the winds seem not to be blowing that way.

Popular Attitudes Toward Atlantic Relations

Before we leave this subject we must look at one more set of data, at a kind of information that will give us a firmer notion of the effect of these trends upon politically important attitudes in the minds of ordinary people. At the same time we can measure another capability for mutual trust and loyalty. We shall study this element through answers to a number of questions asked on attitude surveys (public opinion polls) taken for the United States Information Agency in the major European countries and repeated several times over a period of years. This will give us an opportunity to compare different nations' identification with each other and to trace trends. It cannot provide a measure of elite attitudes, but it will tell us about the opinions of the mass of the population. Also, when we ask people whether they would trust another country as an ally in the case of war, or whether they wish to ally with the West or remain neutral in international relations, we are tapping attitudes of grave political consequence.

Four or five times over a span of nearly a decade the following question was asked in each country: "In case of war, to what extent do you think you could trust [country] as an ally—a great deal, up to a point, or not at all?" Figures 3.1 through 3.3 show the trends, by country, in the percentage answering "a great deal."

The first graph shows the responses of British subjects. Overwhelmingly the United States is most trusted, with a healthy (or unhealthy, as you will) suspicion manifested toward the Continental powers. Appreciably more Britishers trust France than Germany, and the resurgence of West German economic, political, and military power has coincided with a distinct *decline* in British confidence in their ally's trustworthiness. British hostility toward Germany is a fact familiar to all observers of politics in the United Kingdom, and though Britain was never occupied during the war, it is probably greater than current French antipathy to the Germans.

Actually, by 1962 ordinary Britishers' confidence in *all* their allies was notably lower than ten years before. The drop in confidence in America is the least striking, but even it goes from a high of 79 per cent who trusted it "a great deal" in 1952 to only 63 per cent a decade later. Probably this can best be attributed to the changed strategic situation in the early 1960's, as the United States became increasingly vulnerable to Soviet strategic nuclear power, and as there arose greater doubts about America's willingness to risk war in order to protect overseas allies. The decline may also reflect America's action in the Suez crisis of 1956, when the United States sided with the Soviet Union against the British government, on an issue Britain regarded as vital to her security. The steep plummeting of British confidence, in fact, coincides closely with the events in Egypt.

As was the case in Britain, West Germany's confidence in America is far greater than is its confidence in either of its other allies. Unlike Britain, Germany's trust in the United States has risen substantially. In the early postwar years Germany was without military power of her own, and had to depend totally on American protection. Even now, after rearmament, the Federal Republic still is militarily weak and exposed, and a decline in her confidence in America (which

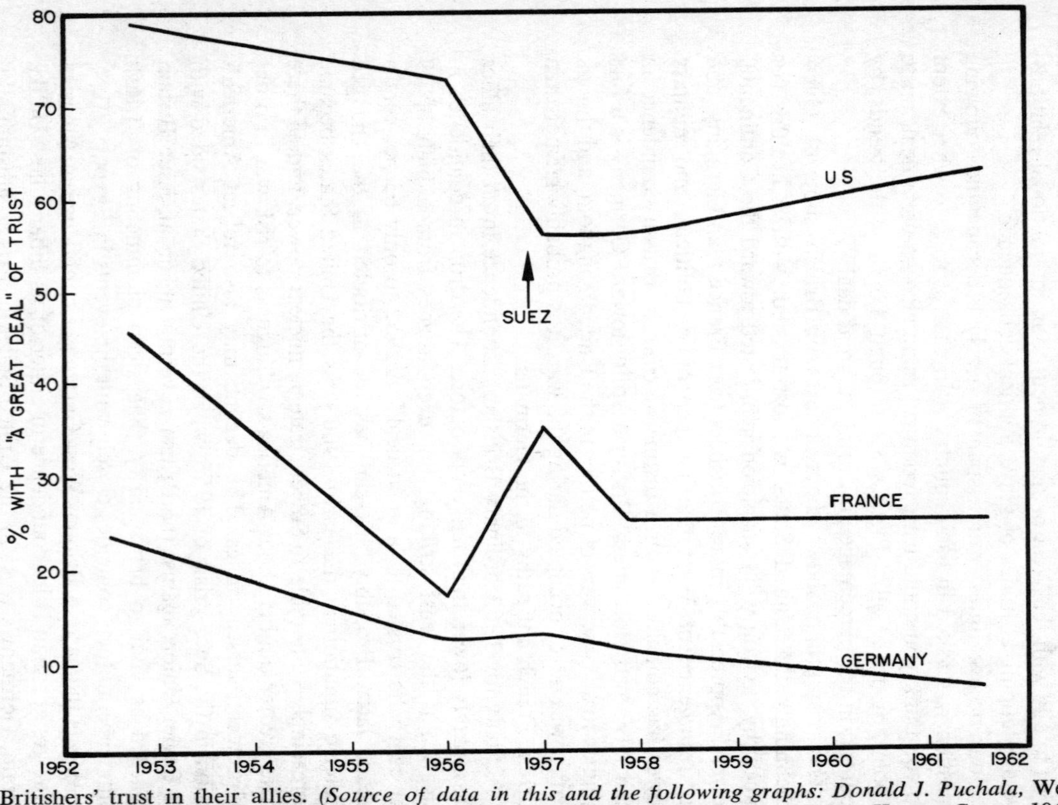

FIGURE 3.1 Britishers' trust in their allies. *(Source of data in this and the following graphs: Donald J. Puchala,* Western European Attitudes on International Problems, *Yale Research Memoranda in Political Science (New Haven, Conn., 1964).)*

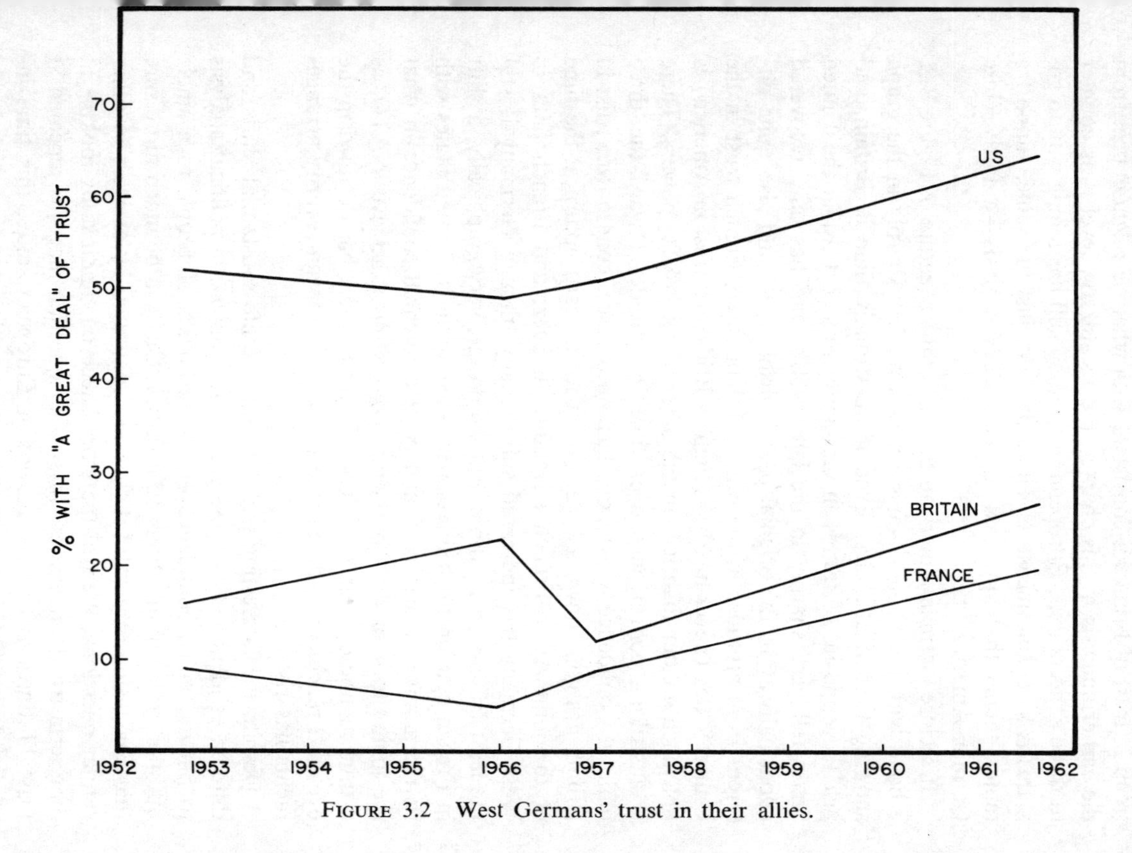

FIGURE 3.2 West Germans' trust in their allies.

fortunately has not appeared) might have the most serious policy consequences. German trust in Britain and France has also risen notably, from a very low level (5 per cent) in the latter case. The trend in trust of France is consistent with what we might expect from the earlier analysis in this chapter, but its still low level runs counter to those expectations. European integration still has a long way to go, if this is a reliable measure. These data do, just the same, support a muted theme that appeared in the earlier analysis—a fairly close German-American tie.

If a close German-American tie was a major feature of Figure 3.2, a bond with the United States emerges far less sharply in the graph showing French attitudes. Even more strongly than in Britain, and just the opposite of trends in Germany, French trust in the United States fell very sharply in the late 1950's, and has only recovered about halfway to the original peak. Furthermore, and also quite different from attitudes in the other two countries, French trust in the United States (never nearly as high as Britishers' trust in America) is not much greater than it is in the other major NATO powers. There is a striking convergence over time in attitudes toward the three nations. Confidence in America has, on balance, gone down; trust in Britain has gone down a little, except for a sharp upturn at the time of the joint Anglo-French adventure in Suez; and French faith in West Germany has increased substantially, though Germany is still the least trusted of the three. But we do see, very graphically, a shift in French opinion toward lesser reliance upon the United States with its thermonuclear deterrent, and greater potential confidence in what the joint efforts of the Continental powers might achieve. NATO, as a transatlantic or even transchannel organization, has declined in the eyes of Frenchmen, whereas the virtue of European security arrangements has risen.

Despite the interesting and sometimes quite substantial shifts and differences identified by these graphs, it is unwise in political analysis to pin too much confidence on the responses of people to a single question or set of questions on a survey. One can be much more sure that conclusions are valid if they are confirmed by answers to other similar questions. We will therefore check our findings by looking at long-term trends in answers to another question that was repeated at least 11 times in each of the major European states, this time including Italy: "At the present time do you think that [country] should be on the side of the West, on the side of the East, or on neither side?" The frequency with which this question was asked allows us

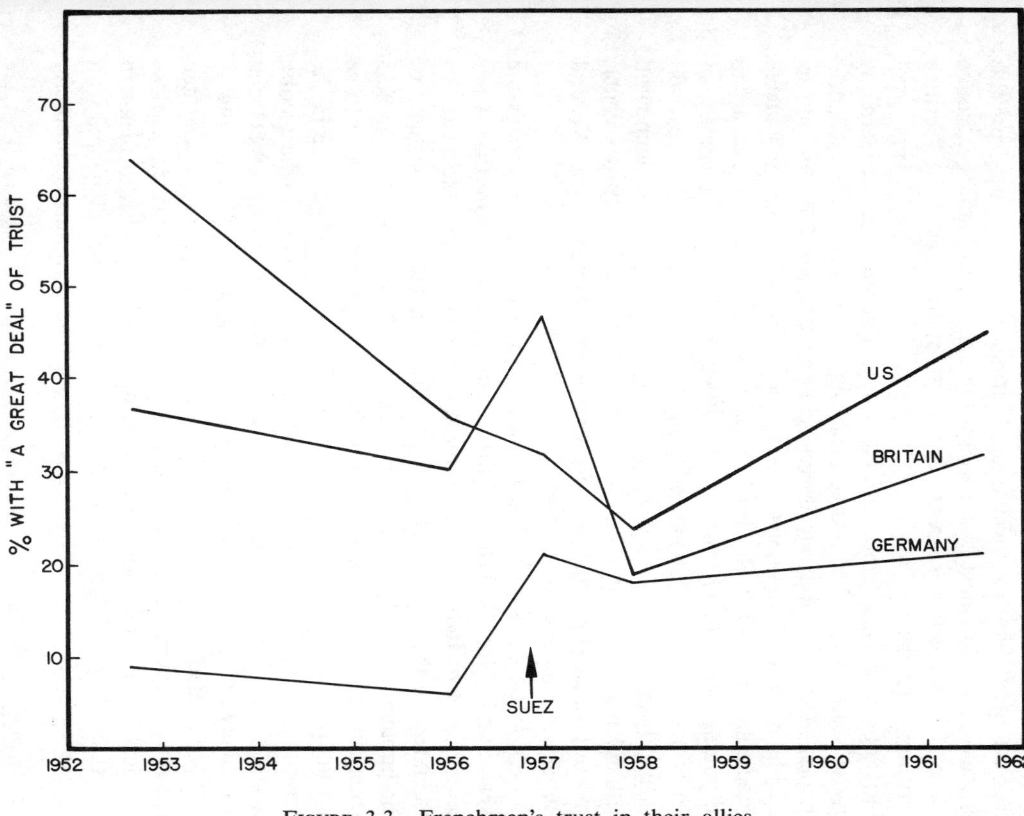

FIGURE 3.3 Frenchmen's trust in their allies.

to be especially confident that the changes over time that we find are not just temporary responses to transient conditions, but rather measure fairly deep and stable attitudes. Figure 3.4 shows the percentage who answered "be on the side of the West."

German attitudes on this matter are remarkably constant, showing, if anything, a slight rise over time.[4] Germany also appears, from this question, to be the most firmly wedded to the Western alliance, though we may nonetheless suspect that a dramatic change in German fortunes, such as the loss of West Berlin, might bring a very great surge of neutralist sentiment. Britain ranks not much below Germany in the proportion of her people professing attachment to the alliance, though there is a moderate decline over time. Even Italy, despite its sizable bloc of Communist voters, shows a fairly high and stable attachment to NATO. But for France, we see both a lower level at the beginning, and a much more unambiguous decline. The percentage of Frenchmen who in 1960 said they should be allied with the West was hardly more than half what it was in 1952 (25 per cent as compared with 42 per cent), only half what it was in Britain (49 per cent), and not much more than a third what it was in the German Federal Republic (62 per cent).

President De Gaulle's influence aside, France is in many ways the weak link in NATO. There is little sentiment (never more than 4 per cent, except in Italy) in any of these countries, France included, for alliance with the Communists. But in France a very large segment of the population, lately twice as large as the NATO "loyalists," prefers a neutral role for the country. The threat of France as a third force is thus perhaps more than an idle one. If we think of France in the context of a neutralist Western European bloc, however, the picture is less clear. West Germany is for now closely bound to NATO and is unlikely to look with favor on alternative policies—providing always that the United States continues to seem capable of protecting German security. Britain, in the improbable event that it formed a close political association with the Continent, would also wish to maintain the alliance with America. Even in Italy the number of people with opinions who favor neutralism is no larger than the number who prefer

[4] Changes of two or three percentage points should be ignored. They are not "statistically significant"; that is, they may be the result only of chance variations in the population sample that was interviewed, and not indicative of any change in the total population. But a shift of four or more percentage points is "significant" at the .05 level, which means that 19 times out of 20 such a difference between two different samples indicates a real shift in the same direction in the population at large.

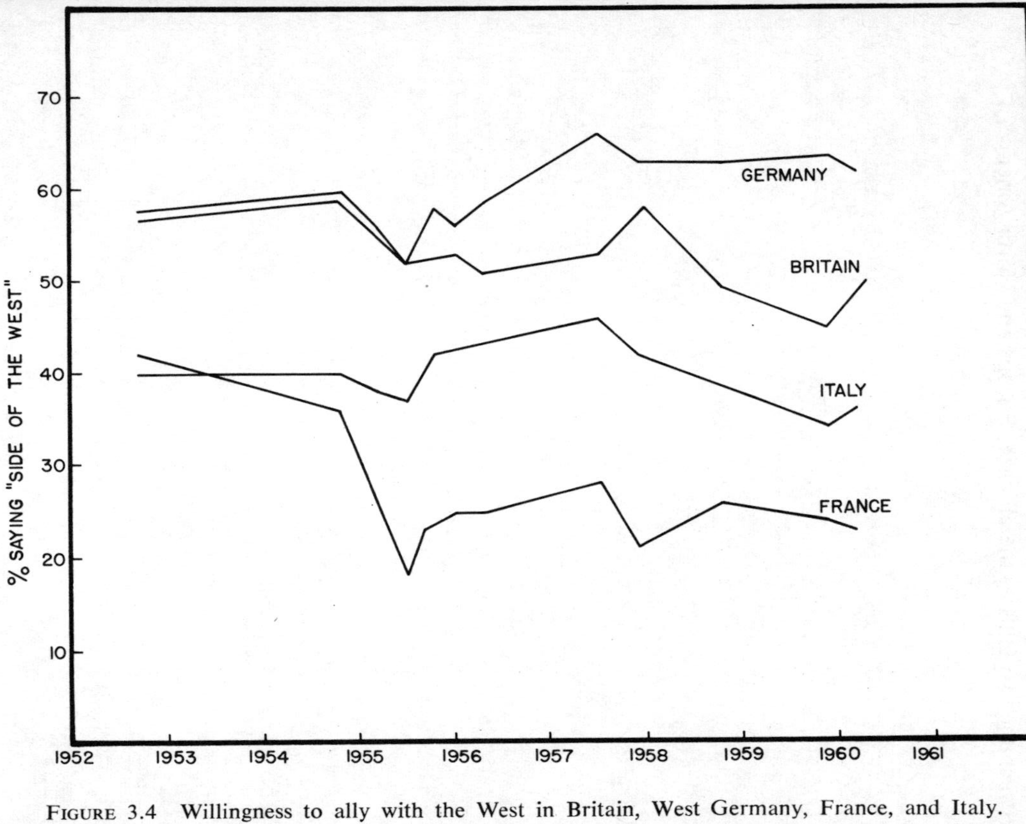

FIGURE 3.4 Willingness to ally with the West in Britain, West Germany, France, and Italy.

NATO. If the other large nations have at least an equal role in foreign policy making, therefore, a united Europe will probably not turn in the direction of a true third force, despite some such tendencies within France. But to the degree that France held the political leadership of a united Europe we might see a distinct loosening of the bond between the two ends of the alliance, Europe and North America.

CHAPTER 4

National Politics and International Politics

Some Similarities

According to the definition of a distinguished American political scientist, a political system "is any persistent pattern of human relationships that involves, to a significant extent, power, rule or authority."[1] This is a very broad definition, because concepts like power, rule, and authority apply not only to national and local governments but to clubs, associations, labor unions, business organizations, perhaps even families, and certainly to the entire world. The world, in international politics, is surely a "pattern of human relationships that involves power, rule and authority."

The most obvious relationship is power—we often speak of the power of various nations to affect the policies of others. Authority, on the other hand, is weak in the international system as a whole. Another famous scholar has labeled authority as "the expected and legitimate possession of power."[2] The United Nations has little authority, because outside of quite narrow limits its members have not assigned legitimate power to it. Nevertheless, it has some authority —such as to require payment of financial assessments—and a majority of its members, acting in concert with decisions in a UN body, can under some circumstances exert considerable power over others. This distinction may perhaps be clearer on reflection about Southern attitudes toward integration in the United States. Many Southerners recognize that the Federal government probably has the *power* to enforce desegregation of public schools, but would contend that it lacks the Constitutional *authority*—that the exercise of its power is not legitimate. In the world, South Africans feel that though the UN

[1] Robert A. Dahl, *Modern Political Analysis* (Englewood Cliffs, N.J.: Prentice-Hall, 1963), p. 6.

[2] Harold D. Lasswell and Abraham Kaplan, *Power and Society* (New Haven, Conn.: Yale University Press, 1950), p. 133.

may have the power to apply sanctions against them, it does not have the authority.

In the absence of substantial authority over its members we find what is probably the greatest difference between politics in the international system and politics within nations. National systems are characterized by institutions empowered to make, execute, and interpret decisions binding on their citizens. Though these institutions are not entirely absent from the international system, they are undeniably weak. But in every society cooperative behavior results not only from the actual or potential threat of sanctions applied by authority. Nor would such institutions guarantee cooperation. In their comparative study of political integration a group of historians and political scientists found the establishment of common governmental institutions and a "monopoly of violence" often more of a hindrance than a help.[3] Of the wars between 1820 and 1949 involving more than 31,000 casualties, at least half were internal rather than international.[4]

Rules of order are often followed, in both local and international society, because of social pressures. A reputation for morality and law-abidingness can be useful, and the contrary reputation damaging. In this respect the United States has an important asset not lightly to be squandered, for with most of its international audience America's word carries a certain presumption of sincerity. Rules may be followed to avoid retaliation by others; retaliation that would damage common interests. Despite their hostility, the United States and the Soviet Union regularly avoid certain forms of threatening behavior (sinking "spying" trawlers, "spoofing" each others radar). On another level, interference with the regular channels of international commerce and postal exchange is generally avoided even though short-term gains might accrue from interference. If a particular case of interference were countered from many sources, all parties might well lose.

Nor is even the threat of retaliation all that restrains a country. Conflict may be eased by agreement about proper procedures or by ethical and moral considerations. It is sometimes fashionable to allege that morality is an illusory force in international relations, but those who characterize world politics as amoral sometimes mistake their own *prescription* for true *description*. As in domestic politics, govern-

[3] Karl W. Deutsch *et al., Political Community and the North Atlantic Area* (Princeton, N.J.: Princeton University Press, 1957), p. 105.

[4] See Lewis F. Richardson, *Statistics of Deadly Quarrels* (Chicago and Pittsburgh: Boxwood Press, 1960), pp. 32–50.

mental leaders are often influenced by moral considerations.[5] Furthermore, what Talcott Parsons calls "an underlying structure of cross-cutting solidarities" produces restraint.[6] Even some firmly anti-Communist governments in Latin America refuse to apply military or economic sanctions to Castro—in part because of their established cultural and political ties with Cuba that cut across the Communist–non-Communist dimension. We shall discuss these and other sources of restraint in the following pages. It simply is erroneous to think of international politics as anarchic, choatic, and utterly unlike national politics. Let us look at some of the similarities, as well as some differences, between national competitive systems and the international system.

As a working hypothesis, subject to rejection if it fails to help us understand reality, the world could be though of as a political system in which the major blocs are analogous to two parties that compete for the favor of the uncommitted voters. Each "party," including a leader and loyal party members of "partisans," tries to convince "voters" that it is best able to fulfill their needs and respect their ethical prescriptions. At this stage of the analysis we shall consider a voter, whether neutral or partisan, as equivalent to the government of a particular nation. The United Nations is, obviously, a major arena of the competition—it is the principal instance where the parties do compete for votes and where the one-nation-one-vote principle holds. In fact, by providing an arena where the parties must participate in a continuing electoral competition for the allegiance of the neutrals, the United Nations contributes in a major way to preserving the system's stability. But the United Nations is not the only arena for this kind of competition. By stretching the analogy somewhat we may extend the case to the competition for foreign military bases and allies. If you are disturbed by the one-nation-one-vote simplification you may imagine some kind of weighted "voting" system at work either inside or outside the Assembly.

In applying these ideas to politics in the General Assembly, a deliberative body, we are making our analogy to domestic politics at the level of the national legislature. Thus our voters are equivalent to

[5] Allegedly a major factor in President Kennedy's decision not to attack Soviet missile bases in Cuba without warning was his conviction that such a course would be morally wrong.

[6] "Order and Community in the International Social System," in James N. Rosenau (ed.), *International Politics and Foreign Policy* (New York: The Free Press, 1961), p. 126.

"elected" representatives who must have a base of power in a local constituency and who ultimately must satisfy (or control) their constituents. But their role as political actors requires them to try to influence other legislators by some combination of bargaining, coercion, and persuasion. Certainly the system is such as to provide some "representatives" with far greater extraparliamentary means of coercing their fellows than is true in national systems. But their ability to achieve their own goals, and to satisfy their constituents, depends heavily on their success in the legislative arena.

As in legislatures, many major votes occur during every session of the Assembly, and equally important opportunities for alignment arise outside the United Nations. These skirmishes are quite comparable to votes in a national legislature; no vote results in the kind of complete victory that would eliminate one of the parties from the electoral process. But there are also important and obvious differences between national systems and the international model suggested here. Perhaps the most significant is the rarity, in the General Assembly, of any victories that could visibly affect the world distribution of power. Whatever the reasons such victories may not occur in national legislatures or in the stalemated larger arena of international conflict, the reason they do not occur in the United Nations is that the representatives in that body have carefully avoided giving it the necessary authority. This encourages use of the Assembly as a propaganda forum as well as an arena for close political bargaining. Many varied interests are represented, but often there is little incentive to force compromise for the achievement of a common parliamentary program, partly because enforcement might be virtually impossible.

Legitimacy and Consensus

Yet despite the differences, which we cannot ignore, let us now examine the similarities somewhat more systematically. Most voters, including all the neutrals and even many of the partisans, prefer a world of continuing competition and no final resolution of the East-West division. They probably have preferences as to the party they would wish to see win in a showdown, but it is far better for their interests, as they see them, that neither party eliminate the other.[7]

[7] For evidence that this applies to partisans as well as to neutrals see Lloyd Free, *Six Allies and a Neutral* (New York: The Free Press, 1959), pp. 33–56. Free cites numerous interviews with members of the Japanese Parliament who affirm their attachment to the Western Alliance but nevertheless believe that

This is not merely because of a fear that final victory would be achieved only by the military destruction of at least one leader, with the simultaneous destruction of many neutrals and partisans. More important, in a competitive world there are many potentialities to be exploited by the voters. Their importance, whether as neutrals or as needed allies, is far greater than their strength would warrant in a world without East-West conflict. Furthermore, they can use their votes on East-West questions to bargain for concessions on other dimensions. Competition between the great powers is likely to produce concessions to the neutrals and the offer of substantial favors like foreign aid, support for anticolonial movements, and help in the achievement of goals such as security from a local enemy. As we shall see below, conditions of competition may also serve to moderate the ideologies or platforms of the major parties; insofar as the original ideology of neither party appeals to the needs of a neutral, this moderating influence should result in a nearer approximation of his wishes.

Not only does competition provide the neutral with parties who become eager suitors for his favor, it provides him with numerous opportunities to seek actively the fulfillment of his wishes. By the promise of his vote, or the implicit or explicit threat to give it to the other party, he may significantly influence the platform or performance of one or both of the parties in his favor. His influence may be dependent upon his ability to maintain his lobby in some kind of uncommitted position. The partisan may, or may not, have substantial control over the politics of his leader; the uncommitted may, by playing his hand shrewdly, influence both leaders.

This is not very different from what goes on in democratic national politics, where neither the neutrals nor, in most cases, even the partisans will aid in the elimination of either party. No matter how deeply committed a party is to achieving final victory over its opponents, when it discovers that victory is not a real possibility for the foreseeable future it must become active in a different kind of politics. The result may be "a delicate negotiating process, with the world organization the forum, not of a community conscience or a concert of power, but of counterbalancing forces unwilling to seek a show-

---

the continuance of East-West competition serves Japanese interests by making the Americans sensitive to Japanese needs. A similar situation surely applies to Poland, including many Polish Communists, who are well aware that even their limited independence is due to the existence of a rival to the Russians.

down, fearful of alienating friends or neutrals, and therefore willing to make concessions." [8]

In domestic politics, of course, stability is maintained not only by a realization that the long-term interests of most voters depend on the maintenance of an effective opposition but by ethical restraints as well. Ideas of what it is *right* to do to one's opponent restrain the partisans. Even Communist parties, in nations where they form a major part of the parliamentary opposition, must at least pay deference to generally accepted ideas of right and wrong.

If the idea of competition and the existence of competing forces is ever to become widely accepted in international politics, it must be through the recognition that all voters share at least some interests in common. A principal mutual interest in the current international arena, though not the only one, is the avoidance of general war. Probably every government can conceive of some conditions that would seem worse than a war, but also of many other outcomes that are definitely more desirable than war. Unavoidably there is considerable overlap of the views of the two sides, so that there are many circumstances both would prefer to general war. The balance of terror, if it remains stable over a long period, may eventually convince each side that it is unable to destroy the other at an acceptable cost. From there, and recognizing their mutual interest in avoiding war, each may eventually develop a sense that the opposition has a legitimate right to exist. One may not approve of the opposition's policies but may grudgingly admit its right to exist and, within limits, to seek adherents. Such a development would be aided by the conscious recognition by the neutrals and many of the partisans that their own interests are best served in a system where two or more opposing parties exist. Some such recognition seems to have occurred in eighteenth- and nineteenth-century England and America.[9] The

[8] Ernst Haas, "Regionalism, Functionalism, and Universal International Organization," *World Politics,* VIII, **2** (January 1956), p. 240. *Cf.* also Haas's comment ("Dynamic Environment and Static System: Revolutionary Regimes in the United Nations," in Morton A. Kaplan, *The Revolution in World Politics* (New York: John Wiley & Sons, 1962), p. 281): "If the Western political process be conceived, not as dispassionate debate, capped by voting and subject to judicial review, but as the articulate defense of rival group interests in permanent confrontation and subject to cumulative compromises, the UN process is not so very different."

[9] Both the Democrats and the Federalists, in the early years of the American republic, regarded themselves as the true interpreters of American doctrine. Only slowly did they become willing to tolerate opposition. *Cf.* William N. Chambers, *Political Parties in a New Nation: The American Experience, 1776–1809* (New York: Oxford University Press, 1963). The peaceful coexistence controversy within the Communist camp does not involve the

existence of the United Nations, and the "right" of the other side to take its case to the world body, may eventually contribute to some such development.

Contact between the two extremes may be maintained by "cross-cutting solidarities." Insofar as voters who adhere to one party belong to or are emotionally attached to organizations including many voters of the other party, this may reduce their demands for fear of losing those with cross-cutting solidarities or by causing disbelief in the ranks about the extremists' charges against the other party. There are rather few of these solidarities between the blocs at present, with the chief exception of Poland's cultural and emotional attachments to the West and Cuba's ties to the Soviet bloc while remaining linked with some Latin American states. On the unofficial level such bonds as those of the Holy See with Roman Catholics in Eastern Europe also should not be ignored. Many more attachments exist, however, between neutrals and members of the two major blocs. They include formal organizations like the Nordic Council and the British Commonwealth, as well as nongovernmental bonds such as Yugoslavia's Communist Party ties and links between neutralist and pro-Western Moslem nations. The role of these cross-cutting solidarities may well expand.

In addition to the effect of various distributions of attitudes among the population, it is important to recognize the effect of various *intensities* of preference. If those who hold the most extreme attitudes also hold them most intensely, a serious threat to the system's stability may exist, especially if the extremists are numerous. The influx of new voters, the emergent nations, into the international arena has meant not only that most voters now prefer a "middle" solution to East-West problems but that most voters are relatively apathetic in a particular sense. That is, the particular issues presented by the two parties' ideologies really have little appeal to them, so that they would not care greatly which was the victor. Their strong preferences are reserved for what are to them private matters—the independence, unification, and development of their own countries, by whatever methods. They are thus not apathetic toward politics in general but merely to the issues presented by the parties. As noted above, in their eyes the achievement of their goals may depend upon the absence of a clear-cut victory for either side. This necessity for two-party competition might, in the long run, be turned into a virtue, as the

---

legitimacy of opposition, but at least turns around the question of whether international politics must be a long-term "system" with "illegitimate" members.

existence of the competitors took on important aspects of legitimacy in the neutrals' eyes.

One is here reminded of the argument, by the authors of a major study of voting behavior in American elections, about the role of the "independent" or, more accurately, the apathetic voter.[10] If the majority of voters held strong preferences the system might quickly become unworkable; only so long as most voters are relatively uninvolved in the ideological arguments of the partisans is the peaceful resolution of conflict possible.

The Distribution of Preferences

Whether the two parties will become more or less extreme in their stands is a crucial question. Currently there is some evidence that the international party leaders have moderated their policies, at least those parts that are explicitly stated. Most of this can be seen as an attempt to win the support of neutrals and to hold that of the less extreme partisans. But whether these developments merely represent temporary tendencies, likely to be reversed in the near future, depends in large part upon the underlying distribution of voters' preferences. This leads to discussion of an influence that could promote system stability but could also lead to the breakdown of the system and either conflict or the emergence of a polycentric system.

As Anthony Downs has shown,[11] *if* most voters are known to favor moderate or middle-of-the-road policies, the two parties' policies will converge toward the center. The possible loss of extremists will not deter the parties' movement toward the center and toward each other, because there will be so few voters to be lost at the margin compared with the number to be gained in the middle. This situation is illustrated in Figure 4.1. The vertical axis measures numbers of voters, and the horizontal axis measures degree of preference for some policy, the extent to which economic control ought to be centralized, for instance, with zero representing no centralization and

[10] Bernard Berelson, Paul F. Lazarsfeld, and William McPhee, *Voting* (Chicago: University of Chicago Press, 1954), pp. 314–315.

[11] *An Economic Theory of Democracy* (New York: Harper & Row, 1957), p. 118. Donald E. Stokes has made a penetrating criticism of the Downs model ("Spatial Models of Party Competition," *American Political Science Review*, LVII [1963], pp. 368–377). Among his points are these: (1) More than one dimension (issue) may be politically relevant, with different preference distributions for each dimension. (2) The salience of various dimensions may change over time. (3) Leaders, partisans, and neutrals all may have different perceptions of salience and preference distributions. These possibilities are, however, dealt with in this and the following chapters.

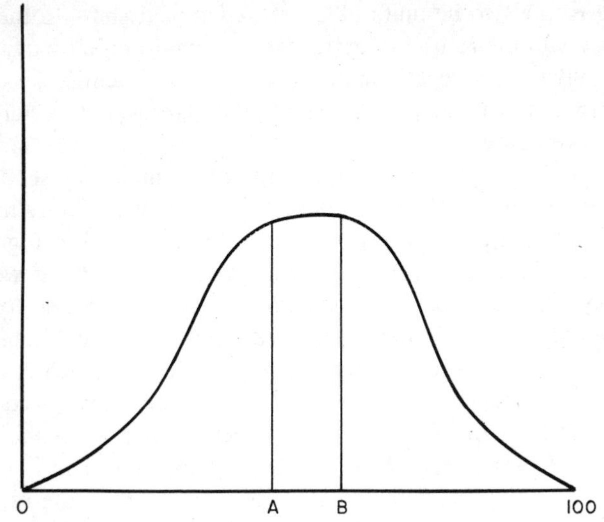

FIGURE 4.1 Two-party convergence when preferences are distributed unimodally.

100 complete central control. If voters' preferences are such that most voters are found at a single mode around 50, then both party A and party B will tend, over time, to move toward that mode.

But if preferences are distributed bimodally, as in Figure 4.2, the

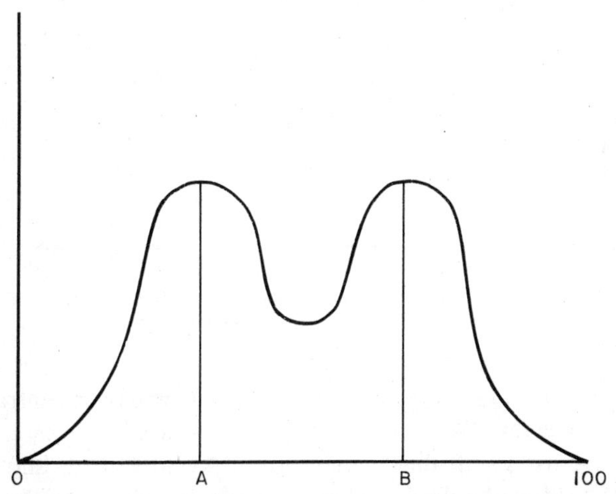

FIGURE 4.2 Two-party divergence when preferences are distributed bimodally.

outcome is likely to be quite different. Attempted shifts to the center may meet with the refusal of extremists to support either party if both become alike or at least similar. Because the potential loss at the margin to a third party is so great, the parties may retain quite different programs.

The recent moderation that a few observers think they see in some of the two international parties' policies on East-West issues might be traced to a world preference pattern like that indicated in Figure 4.1, which the parties have just now begun to recognize. But if we introduce a dynamic element, any moderation may be traceable to a shift in the world preference pattern caused by the "enfranchisement" of new voters. As the African and Asian countries have achieved independence and admission to the United Nations they have become new voters for whom the parties must compete. Whereas at the end of World War II preferences were distributed bimodally as in Figure 4.2, by the end of the 1950's the addition of new voters to the ranks had created another peak toward the center.

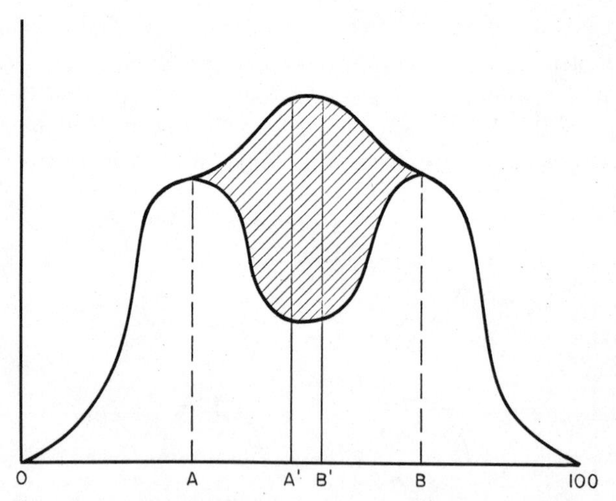

FIGURE 4.3 Two-party convergence with the creation of a single center mode by the enfranchisement of new voters.

Figure 4.3 above illustrates one possible outcome of the enfranchisement of new voters. With the emergence of a new single mode at the center, the parties shift their policies from A and B to A′ and B′. But the result need not be the one above, for the size of the center mode is crucial. If it were much smaller, not significantly higher than the modes at A and B and separated from each of the original peaks by a valley, the most likely outcome would be not the convergence of A and B but the creation of a third party, a "neutral bloc" C.

Any of these outcomes can of course occur only if both parties actually play the parliamentary game; that is, only if both do in fact seek to achieve voting majorities. This need not happen in the international system so long as either side retains some hope of attaining its majority through extraparliamentary methods, as by picking off opposing states one by one through subversion. In the period from 1957 to 1959 Moscow seems actually at times to have regarded the UN as an organization it might eventually come to control. Later events, especially the Russians' inability to direct the Congo operation, burst this bubble. But on several occasions, once its defeat on a resolution sponsored by the underdeveloped countries was clear, Moscow ceased its opposition. Sometimes when it could not win on a particular issue it backed down from an extreme position which might have prejudiced its efforts to win majorities on other issues. If it were to give up serious attempts to win majorities—and thus lose a major incentive to adopt moderate centristic stances—there would be no reason to look for two-party convergence. One party, such as the West led by the United States, might indeed move toward the middle to pick up votes without encouraging similar behavior by its opponent. In such a case the average position of the whole Assembly would shift eastward, but the attitude distribution would remain bimodal. Some assessments of the current international situation would argue that this is roughly what has happened, and in the following chapters we shall examine our data with this possibility, as well as more hopeful ones, in mind.

A World of Many Issues

We have been speaking largely as though there were only one basic alignment. As we shall see, an "East versus West" voting pattern is by far the most common one in the General Assembly. Nevertheless, there are other alignments that often appear. Sometimes, for instance, most of the states of Western Europe join with the Soviet Bloc to vote against the underdeveloped countries—a kind of North-South alignment.

If many different kinds of issues are considered in the UN, on votes which show different kinds of alliances, this should, in the long run, contribute to stabilizing the system. While the United States saw the UN primarily as a forum for promoting Western Cold War interests, the independents and neutral-leaning partisans found themselves in a relatively weak bargaining position. But now, with the greater prominence of economic development and self-determination as major issues in their own right, many nations have substantial freedom of maneuver. They may bargain and engage in logrolling, exchanging support on security issues for votes against colonialism. As the authors of *The American Voter* declare:

> If an electorate responds to public affairs in terms of one or a few well-defined and stable ideological dimensions on which there is little movement of opinion, political controversy will be relatively tightly bounded and the possibilities of party maneuver . . . relatively circumscribed. But if an electorate responds to public affairs in a less structured fashion, politics will be more fluid, party strategy will include or may consist primarily of exploiting new dimensions of opinion, and the likelihood of party alternation in power will be greater.[12]

The emergence of new issues might eventually contribute to a sharp increase in the number of issues that are characterized by a North-South alignment. It has been alleged that America, Western Europe, and the Soviet Bloc may someday decide that they share a common interest in preserving their wealth from confiscation by an aroused underdeveloped bloc. This could conceivably produce the emergence of a new have-not party, followed by the merger of the former opponents into a single party. Or it might mean simply that the voting alignment on some types of issues would be radically different from that on other matters.

An increase in the variety of issues could contribute in other ways. A cumulative pattern of compromises and concessions can set up expectations of peace, stability, and co-existence that may restrain the leaders. Even if the leaders make concessions purely as temporary expedients and not out of any desire to promote such expectations, they are likely to give rise to hopes that it will be costly to disappoint.

The rise of issues other than the Cold War may make it possible for some partisans even of the tightly organized Communist bloc occasionally to deviate from the basic party position. One can hardly imagine that the Soviets would tolerate deviation on a major Cold War threat in the near future, but on some other matters a vote against the Bloc, or an abstention, might possibly be overlooked. By providing opportunities for deviation on issues that are not central to the Soviet Union's security we may contribute to a wholesome precedent. Once deviation is tolerated at all it may be difficult to stop it short of a certain fluidity even on rather vital matters.

[12] A. Campbell, P. Converse, W. Miller, and D. Stokes, *The American Voter* (New York: John Wiley & Sons, 1960), p. 550.

CHAPTER 5

Trends in UN Politics

Measuring Attitudes and Intensities

We must now have a look at what the basic issues and voting alignments in the UN really are. To do so we shall study who votes how on roll-call (recorded) votes in the Assembly. Roll-call votes provide an especially useful means of identifying states' attitudes. They occur on a very wide variety of issues, they are numerous, and they force a state to take a position. (A country may of course abstain or be absent, but just the avoidance of a clear pro or con position gives valuable information.) There are difficulties, too, in using roll-call votes. We have no fully satisfactory way of deciding which roll calls are more important than others, though we can at least eliminate repetitive votes on, for instance, different paragraphs of the same resolution. Nor strictly from the roll calls is it possible to know how strongly a state feels about a particular position. A Latin-American state might vote with the United States for reasons other than its attitude toward the issue immediately at stake. But there are ways of easing these difficulties, especially for evaluating the intensity of attitudes, as we shall see below.

In our basic examination of issues and voting alignments we shall rely upon the results of a technique known as factor analysis. All votes (yes, no, abstain) are recorded and analyzed in a high-speed electronic computer. Very simply, what factor analysis does here is pick out all roll calls that have a similar underlying voting pattern, such as votes that find the West and the Soviet Bloc opposed, or votes where the Soviets and Western Europeans together oppose the underdeveloped countries. Each of these basic alignments would be identified as representing a different "factor," or underlying "superissue." The technique allows us to discover both how many such different alignments there actually are and to find the frequency of each. It provides a statistic (labeled lambda) that expresses the percentage of variation on all roll calls in the Assembly that is accounted for by a particular factor or superissue. Also, after identifying the factors we can locate particular nations on those factors by deriving "factor scores." The factor scores tell us how pro-West, or pro-East, any given country is. Finally, and most important, the method is completely *objective*. The assignment of a country to a position on the East-West continuum is determined by that country's own voting pattern, not on the subjective assessment of some outside observer.

The technique of factor analysis has been applied to votes in four different sessions of the UN General Assembly: those beginning in 1947, 1952, 1957, and 1961.[1] One of the most striking results was the continuity in UN concerns. Two major factors or superissues appeared in every session, and they have been labelled according to the rough similarity between countries' factor scores on them and their geographical locations in the world.

The most common alignment has been called "East-West" because of the content of the issues of which it is composed and because of the pattern of countries' factor scores. Some of the particular issues that were characterized by this alignment were votes condemning racial discrimination in South Africa and votes on Arab refugees in Palestine, UN membership for Communist China, disarmament, Hungary, Korea, Indonesian efforts to take over former Netherlands New Guinea, and several African "colonialism" questions; that is, votes concerning the independence of former colonial peoples. Neither South African nor Palestine questions fit this latter description perfectly, but there still are strong elements of similarity both in the substance of the issues and in the voting patterns. The Soviet Bloc and the allies of the United States are at opposite ends of this continuum, as one might expect. Latin Americans and especially West Europeans vote much like the United States on these matters, but they are not quite so far "West"—in other words, on some issues they occasionally vote against the United States or abstain. There are also a few very pro-Western Asians, usually American military allies like Taiwan, Japan, Thailand, and the Philippines. Iran and Pakistan are near the middle, but most Asians and Arabs are farther "East," though never quite so far as the Soviet Union and its satellites. The new states of Africa, especially the former French colonies, tend to be only slightly East of the center.

It is very important to remember that East-West here means not just Cold War issues like admitting Red China to the UN, but also the colonialism votes. In other words, because an Afro-Asian country

[1] For more data on these sessions and a full description of factor analysis and its application to voting patterns in the United Nations see Hayward R. Alker, Jr., and Bruce M. Russett, *World Politics in the General Assembly* (New Haven, Conn.: Yale University Press, 1965).

is found far to the East does not mean that it is voting East because the Russians want it to. Sometimes this is true on Cold War issues, but on colonial self-determination issues it is basically the Afro-Asians who lead the fight. The Russians go along and do their best to intensify the conflict and alienate the Afro-Asians from the West, but the anti-Western position of many non-Communist states on these issues is not dependent upon the Soviet stand.

"North-South" is the second most important dimension, so-called because the Communist–Western allies distinction is basically irrelevant and it essentially pits the developed countries against the underdeveloped ones. Roll-call votes which make up this dimension include votes on nuclear testing (with neutrals condemning tests by all major powers), economic aid to developing nations, and a number of votes about financing the UN Emergency Force in the Congo. The Russians originally agreed to the Congo Force, but when it turned out not to serve their interests they joined with some of the European colonial powers, like France, in a refusal to pay assessments to meet its expenses. It is an alliance of those who are most opposed to enlarging the powers of the world body, especially when it seems likely that those powers would be used against their interests. It also includes a strong element of resistance to Afro-Asian attempts to channel larger sums of foreign aid through the UN. On this dimension overall, the most Northern states are South Africa (the target of some of the most extreme North-South initiatives) and France, followed closely by the Soviet bloc. Other Western Europeans are fairly far up toward the North, with the United States about in the middle of them. Most Latin Americans and Asians are South of the "equator," with Africa furthest South.

Two quite striking things occur on this dimension—China (Taiwan), probably as a consequence of its dependence on American support, is much farther North than any other Asian country, and Yugoslavia, though very East, is far from the Soviet bloc on North-South votes. Because these are, to the Russians, important issues (the Congo affair, as it worked out, seriously disillusioned them about their prospects for using the UN to further important Soviet foreign policy aims), it is highly misleading to think of Yugoslavia as just another Russian satellite.

Remember that these voting patterns are not something peculiar to the 1961 Assembly session but have been there virtually since the beginning of the UN. The particular issues to be voted on have varied somewhat, but the basic alignments have not. We said that the factor analysis provides a statistic, lambda, which expresses the percentage of all variation in voting that is accounted for by a particular superissue. In the four sessions analyzed, East-West issues accounted for about 45 per cent of the interpretable variation in 1947, 51 per cent in 1952, 64 per cent in 1957, and 68 per cent in 1961. North-South issues, the second most common set, accounted for about 20 per cent of the interpretable variation in 1947 and 1952, 15 per cent in 1957, and 13 per cent in 1961. Together they account for between two thirds and four fifths of the voting. Most states have retained their basic positions on these alignments, though the Latin Americans have, over time, moved somewhat Northwest. The admission of about 50 new Afro-Asian states since 1947, however, has more than compensated for the Latin shift.

In terms of our theoretical interests outlined in the previous chapter, we now have a way of measuring the distribution of nations' *attitudes* on different issues, but still need an index of the *intensity* with which they hold those attitudes. One way of finding out which governments felt most strongly about a given issue would have been simply to ask their delegates. But for events 10 or 15 years ago delegates' familiarity with their governments' policies, and their memories, simply could not be trusted. Another solution would be to look at the behavior of the delegates as recorded in the official record. Who speaks most often on a given topic? We could count the number of speeches by each national delegation on all the individual issues that made up a particular superissue in the factor pattern, with the assumption that those who hold an attitude most intensely will speak most often.

There are some flaws in this solution. The major powers, especially the United States and the Soviet Union, tend to speak frequently on virtually everything. Thus we would find, with this measure, that the major powers were most "intense" on everything, and this is probably not really true. Second, talkativeness may be a personality trait of the delegate, not an indicator of conviction. A single cogent, powerful, carefully prepared speech may indicate a far deeper concern than several casually delivered addresses.

To check for this kind of misleading effect we also constructed an index of intensity that was based on whether or not a state even voted, whether its delegates spoke on the issue and how often, and whether they introduced resolutions or amendments on the topic, and compared the results from this index with those of the simple speech count. The result was a very high correlation of $r = .88$. (The correlation coefficient, r, is a common measure of association. It may vary from 0 to 1.00, with the former indicating no association and the latter perfect correlation. When squared it gives the percentage of total variation in one measure that can be explained by the other. In this case, the $r^2 = .80$, a very high figure in most social science.) A comparison of the speech count alone with the introduction of resolutions and amendments alone also produced very similar results. This indicated that we would get roughly the same picture with any of these possible indices of intensity, and so we used the one that was simplest to compile, the number of speeches.

Now it is nevertheless true that the results are not identical, and that any simple measure like this (and also the use of roll-call votes described earlier) will distort the "real" picture somewhat. But we must remember that we are looking for an *objective,* fairly precise index. A scientific endeavor requires results that can be duplicated by another researcher who tries to apply the same criteria to the same data. This quality is sometimes called "replicability," and makes it possible for other scientists to check the original researcher's work to be sure it was well done and to see just where it might be modified or improved. Without this quality a reader cannot be quite sure how much confidence he should place in a writer's conclusions. The argument may be strong and well made, and the writer may have a long record of perceptive observation. But another perceptive writer might reach different conclusions. Contrast the two old saws, both of which are persuasive: "Absence makes the heart grow fonder." "Out of sight, out of mind." Which is correct? When? How? How do we know? By attempting to construct precise indices to measure political phenomena we lose detail, we perhaps lose some of the spark and deep insight that a less rigorous approach might provide, but we expect to counter that loss with the greater certainty that we can attach to the conclusions we do reach.

A famous sociologist, Paul Lazarsfeld, has discussed the problems involved in trying to construct indices:

> Each individual indicator has only a probability relation to what we really want to know. A man might maintain his basic position, but by chance shift on an individual indicator; or he might by chance remain stable on a specific indicator. But if we have many such indicators in an index, it is highly unlikely that a large number of them will change in one direction, if the man we are studying has in fact not changed his basic position.[2]

[2] Paul F. Lazarsfeld, "Evidence and Inference in Social Research," in Daniel Lerner (ed.), *Evidence and Inference* (New York: The Free Press, 1959), p. 104.

Thus we compare different indices to see if they give essentially the same results. And we apply the indices to different bodies of data (in this case to four different sessions of the Assembly). While we are of course looking to see if there is any change in the picture as measured by our indices, at the same time we expect a certain continuity from one year to the next, or at least that the apparent changes will be ones for which we can find a reasonable theoretical explanation. Finally, it is always useful to compare results with those obtained by a less rigorous impressionistic analysis. It is not true that one's findings should always correspond with common sense—some of the most exciting moments in scientific work come when common sense is contradicted. But if informed sensitive observers disagree violently with the results of your analysis it pays to find out why. Accordingly, a major part of the research project described in these chapters consisted of interviewing UN diplomats to discover their impressions of the situation.

Alignments and Intensities

We suggested in the last chapter that for various reasons the stability of the international system would be increased if there were many different issues and alignments, implying a partial shift away from the East-West split. On page 70 we indicated that the East-West alignment has become more pervasive, not less so. It accounted for 45 per cent of the interpretable variation in roll-call voting in 1947, and this rose to 68 per cent in 1961. The second most common factor, the North-South one, declined from 20 per cent to 13 per cent over the same period. To put it another way, in 1947 the East-West alignments were twice as common as North-South alignments; by 1961 they were five times as common. By 1961 the East-West confrontation had come to dominate the Assembly in a way it had not done previously. There is no evidence of an emerging alliance between the West and Communist haves against the underdeveloped have-nots—in fact, quite the contrary.

Issues that in earlier years had appeared on the North-South factor turned up on the East-West dimension in 1961. Palestine, a major component of the North-South dimension in 1947, is a striking example. Here most of the change can be traced to the shift of the Soviet Union from pro-Israel in 1947 to a militantly pro-Arab position in later years. Also, in earlier years some at least of the colonialism issues appeared on the North-South dimension: a UN Trusteeship for the island of Nauru in 1947, independence for Morocco and Somaliland in 1952, a few votes on the Cameroons and South Africa in 1957. But of all the colonialism votes in 1961, only two votes on the Belgian presence in the African territory of Ruanda-Urundi were characterized by a North-South alignment.

Another way of measuring pervasiveness is to count the frequency of speech making on an issue. In 1947 and 1952 approximately twice as many speeches were made on East-West as on North-South issues. By 1957 the ratio rose to three to one, and by 1961 five times as many speeches were made on East-West issues as on North-South problems. These data on frequency of speeches almost exactly parallel our data on frequency of votes.

It is difficult to explain these striking findings in the light of common assertions that the North-South conflict is a new one, a dimension that has only recently come into prominence. Because these assertions are usually made by Americans, perhaps the viewpoint may be traced to a peculiarly American outlook on world politics—the United States is newly concerned with North-South issues. Figure 5.1 indicates America's new concern with North-South questions. It shows trends over time in the number of speeches made both by the average UN member and by the United States on both East-West and North-South issues.

The United States has always been far more interested in both North-South and East-West issues than the average UN member. In 1947 and in 1961 it made about four times as many speeches as the average member on East-West issues, and about two and one half the average in the intervening years. But on North-South issues its score was, until 1961, only about twice that of the average member. In 1961, however, it rose to a level between five and six times the average.

Through 1957 the United States was able to get its way on East-West issues with relative ease. By 1961, however, it sometimes had to work quite hard to achieve its accustomed majority. Paradoxically, the difficulty in rounding up votes on East-West issues may be at the root of the greater interest in North-South problems. To get support on things it thinks important the United States has had to bargain and has had to show more concern regarding issues that are important to other states. As the United States delegation begins to take a new interest in North-South issues, American analysts begin, for the first time, to notice a voting alignment that has in fact existed since the beginning of the organization. Nevertheless, the relative emphasis on

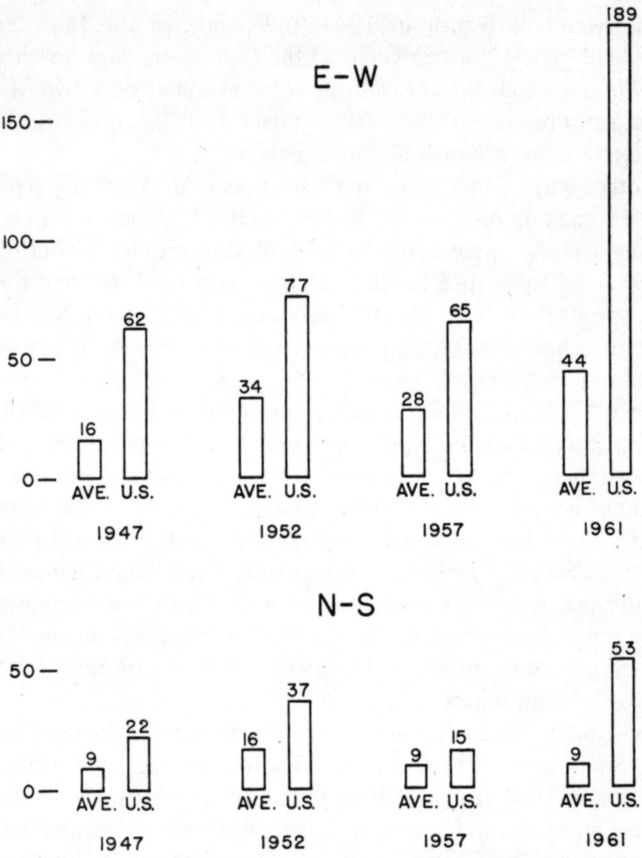

FIGURE 5.1 Speeches on East–West and North–South issues.

North-South issues, both in number of speeches and in number of votes, has declined rather sharply. East-West issues have increased significantly. The polarization of attitudes in the General Assembly is on the upswing, not on the decline.[3]

[3] One qualification to this conclusion stems from our use of speeches and roll-call votes. On a few highly divisive issues there is evidence that both sides endeavor to prevent the topic from reaching a formal vote. The neutrals now try very hard to exclude strictly Cold War issues from Assembly consideration, and particularly to avoid Cold War divisions where the United States and the Soviets vote on opposite sides. On subjects like nuclear testing their aim is to produce resolutions on which both great powers will vote in favor or abstain. Thus the Cold War dimension was relatively infrequently represented in our analysis of the Sixteenth Session partly because of the neutrals' efforts not to have it discussed. Similarly, the underdeveloped countries, in their ad-

But to modify this gloomy conclusion there are trends in the distribution of East-West issues between Cold War and colonial self-determination questions that suggest a greater chance of a stable system. By a procedure known as "rotating" the factors[4] we can distinguish the content of different kinds of issues that appear on the unrotated factor. Most important in this case, we can separate Cold War issues from self-determination ones. Both appear on the unrotated East-West factor, but the voting alignments on each actually are somewhat different. Again we can talk about the percentage of variation (lambda) accounted for by each factor.

Cold War and self-determination alignments were not yet distinguishable in 1947, even on the rotated factor pattern. But by 1952 they could be separated, and Cold War issues accounted for 11 per cent of the interpretable variation; in 1957 the Cold War rose to 29 per cent; and in 1961 it fell back again to 19 per cent.

A far clearer indication of this trend, however, is the relative decline in speech making on the Cold War. Figure 5.2 shows speeches by the United States, the Soviet Union, and the Assembly average for the three years in which Cold War and self-determination have been distinct.

The increasing boredom of the Assembly with Cold War issues stands out. The Americans and the Soviets delivered more than twice as many speeches on Cold War issues in 1961 as in 1952; after a brief rise in 1957 the average General Assembly member actually gave fewer Cold War speeches in 1961 than in 1952. The ratio of the Soviet-American score to the average score rose from about three to one in 1952 to eight to one in 1961.

Further support for this argument comes from making a ratio of speeches on any superissue to the percentage of interpretable variation in the voting accounted for by that issue dimension. The result is a kind of over-all intensity score for the entire membership, with speech making weighted by each issue's pervasiveness in Assembly voting. We find that between 1952 and 1961 this "intensity score" rose by about 50 per cent or more for most of the major unrotated and rotated dimensions (from 40 to 65 for East-West, 48 to 70 for North-

---

vocacy of a Special United Nations Fund for Economic Development (SUNFED) worked ardently to avoid a roll-call vote all during the years when it was under discussion. They knew they could win a vote but could not implement it against the wishes of the major contributors.

[4] For an explanation of the procedure see Alker and Russett, *op. cit.*, Chs. 2 and 3.

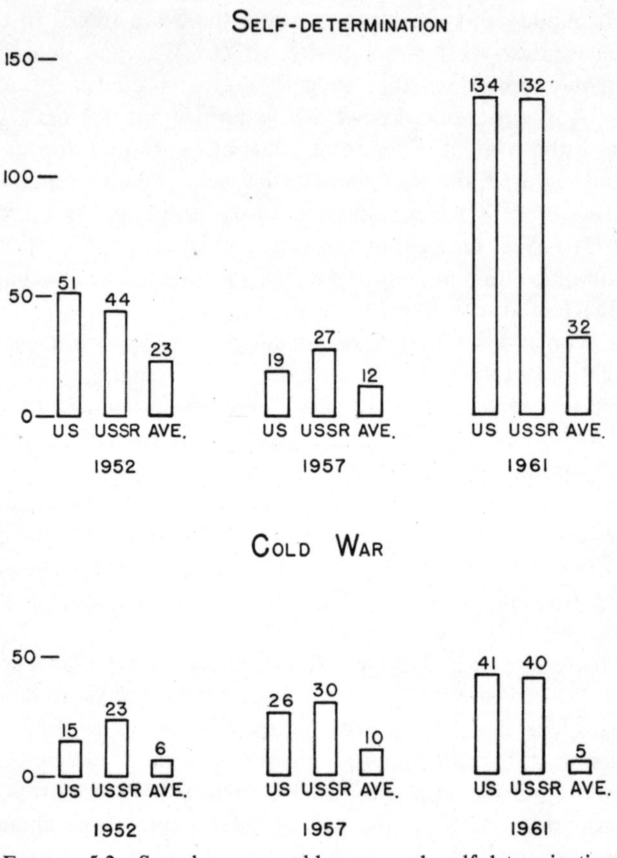

FIGURE 5.2 Speeches on cold war and self-determination issues.

South, and 48 to 83 for self-determination). The trend has been toward more speeches per issue—a consequence, perhaps, of the enlarged membership of the Assembly. But for Cold War issues the trend in "intensity scores" has been *downward*; the index has declined from 33 to 27. Not only have the underdeveloped states been very successful in preventing Cold War issues from coming to a vote in the UN, they even have to a large degree discouraged the *discussion* of such matters in the international forum.

As implied by the over-all "intensity scores," a different trend is discernible on self-determination issues. Instead of declining, the mean number of speeches has risen by nearly 50 per cent since 1952. In 1961 the average Assembly delegation talked six and one half times as much about self-determination problems as about Cold War issues. Although they delivered eight times as many speeches as the average member on Cold War issues, the Russian and American speech totals were only four times greater than average on self-determination. But even this marks a substantial increase, as the major powers themselves were forced, in order to hold the attention of other states, to devote much more of their attention to the Assembly's preoccupation with self-determination and end of colonialism.

This greater boredom with the Cold War is not due primarily to the admission of new African states. It is true that in 1961 there were far more African states than previously and that collectively they showed the same low level of interest in the Cold War as Ethiopia and Liberia had nine years previously. But as can be seen in Table 5.1, with the exception of the two superpowers, every group showed

Table 5.1 Speeches per Issue

	1952		*1957*		*1961*	
	C W	*S-D*	*C W*	*S-D*	*C W*	*S-D*
United States	15	51	26	19	41	134
U.S.S.R.	23	44	30	27	40	132
West Europeans	5	26	9	11	4	37
Latin Americans	4	16	6	12	3	20
Soviet Satellites	11	18	11	10	8	26
Asians	5	23	14	13	8	36
Arabs	4	27	7	9	3	37
Africans	2	26	11	11	2	33

a lower level of interest in the Cold War in 1961 than in 1957, and in most cases lower than in 1952. This is true not only of the neutrals but of the West Europeans and the Soviet Satellites.

We suggested in the previous chapter that bloc, or party, leaders would increasingly be forced to turn away from Cold War issues if they were to retain their influence among the mass of "voters." That development has not yet occurred, but the forces that would produce it are plainly evident. It seems plausible to expect that the current lag will at least in part be made up and that the bloc leaders will, like their followers, in time shift their public emphasis from Cold War issues to the kind of problem on which they are likely to strike a more sympathetic chord in the Assembly.

The Role of the Middleman

In the previous chapter we set forth the hypothesis that, "If those who hold the most extreme attitudes also hold them most intensely, a serious threat to the system's stability may exist, especially if the extremists are numerous." The converse might read: For the system to be stable there should be a body of neutrals who are relatively intense about their neutralism; that is, who maintain a middle position and who do so with some degree of involvement, with an active effort to uncover grounds of agreement between the extremes and produce solutions on those grounds. And the smaller the body of such neutrals is, the more intense must be their commitment to a middle ground if they are to exert a significant stabilizing effect. The next two sets of graphs, Figures 5.3 and 5.4, give us a chance first to compare the *size* of the middle group with the groups at either extreme, on both the East-West and the North-South dimensions. Other information on the same graphs will show the *intensity* of the different groups' attitudes.

First, let us look at attitudes on the East-West issues as shown in Figure 5.3. These graphs resemble the curves presented in the previous chapter, except that, instead of being hypothetical, they are drawn from the actual data. Across the horizontal axis appear the factor scores, or positions of various countries on East-West ques-

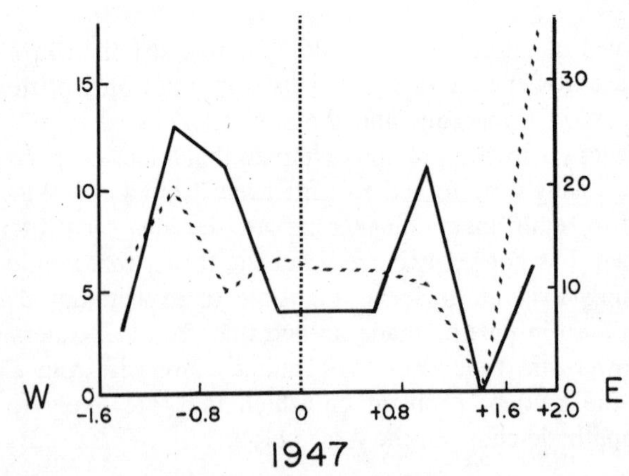

FIGURE 5.3 Distribution of East–West attitudes and intensities.

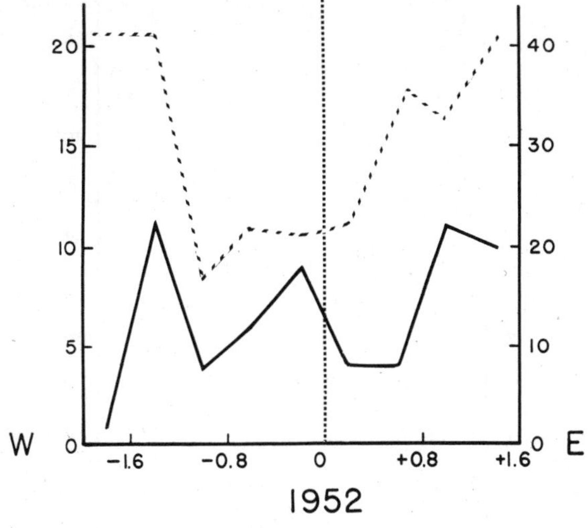

FIGURE 5.3B

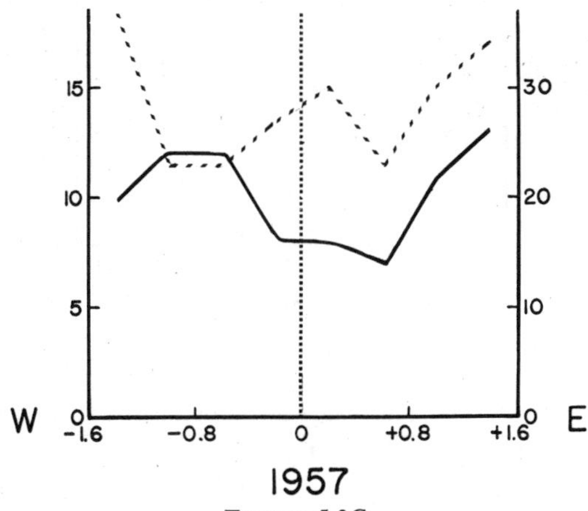

FIGURE 5.3C

tions. Zero, marked by a dashed *vertical* line, is the average factor score. Along the vertical axis marked on the *left* is the *number of countries;* on the vertical axis marked on the *right* is the average *intensity* of attitude, the mean number of speeches on topics that appear as part of the given superissue. The jagged *solid* line represents the distribution of attitudes, the number of states within each

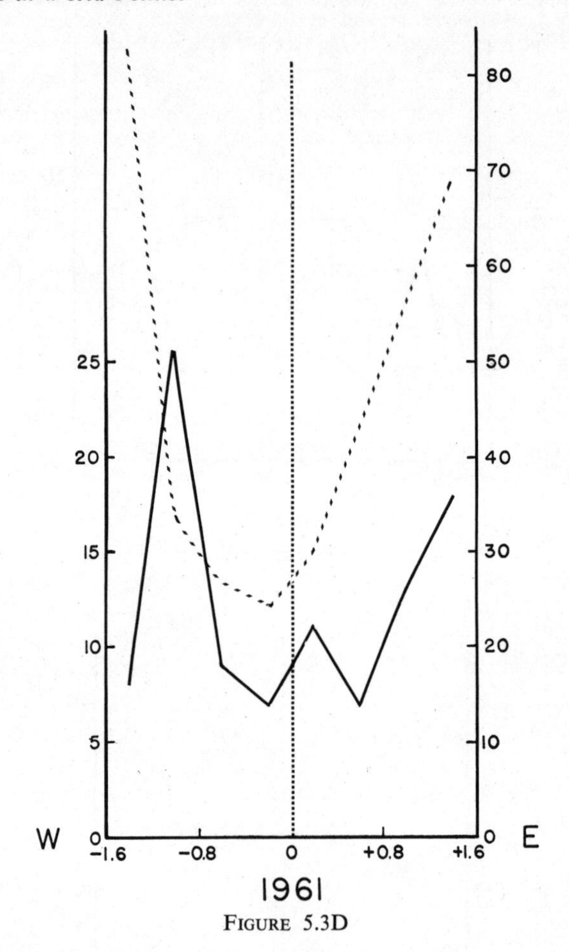

FIGURE 5.3D

range of factor scores. The jagged *dashed* line shows the average intensity for states within that range. We shall look first at the *solid* jagged lines for the distribution of factor scores.

In Figure 5.3 one sees a fairly clear case of a "three-party" system. Throughout the period since 1947 there has been a substantial "middle" group on East-West issues, usually located somewhat to the East of center. But the relative size of this center group has been declining quite steadily—particularly as the East's voting strength has grown. Furthermore, the composition of the center "party" has been far from constant. In 1947 the "central" peak (actually well to the East of center) represents the position of India, most Arabs, and some other Afro-Asians. By 1952 these same Afro-Asians are to be found in a position nearly as East as the Soviet bloc, and they stay substantially there from then on. Their place as a "center" group is taken mostly by Latin Americans in 1952 (West of center this time), by a mixed group of Latins, Asians, and some Arabs in 1957, and substantially by the newly admitted Brazzaville Africans in 1961. For purposes of UN voting, at least, the particular group of Afro-Asians typified by Egypt, India, and Indonesia is not a moderating center group on most East-West issues. Rather it makes up, with the Soviet bloc, the Eastern "party." The central, balancing group is to be found elsewhere—and it is diminishing in size.

Figure 5.4 allows us to make the same kind of analysis of North-

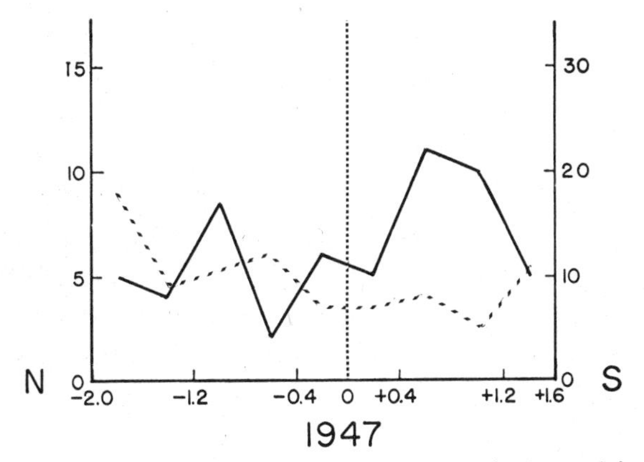

FIGURE 5.4 Distribution of North–South attitudes and intensities.

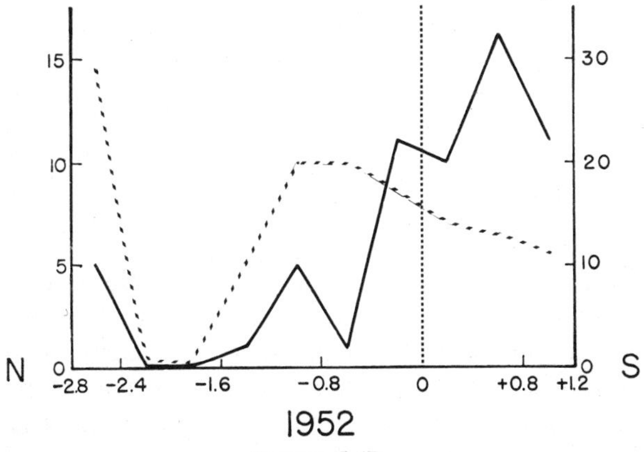

FIGURE 5.4B

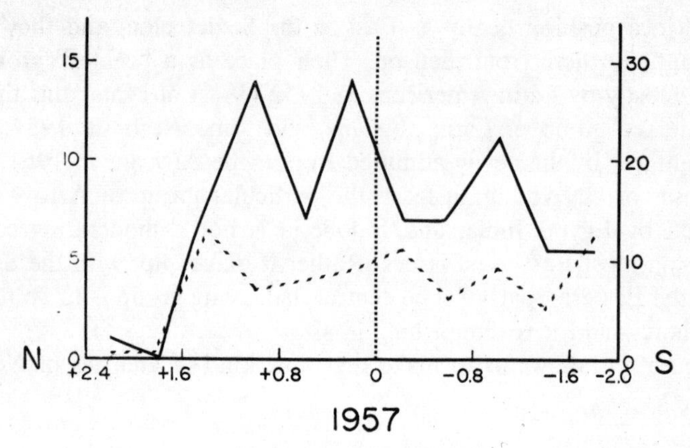

FIGURE 5.4C

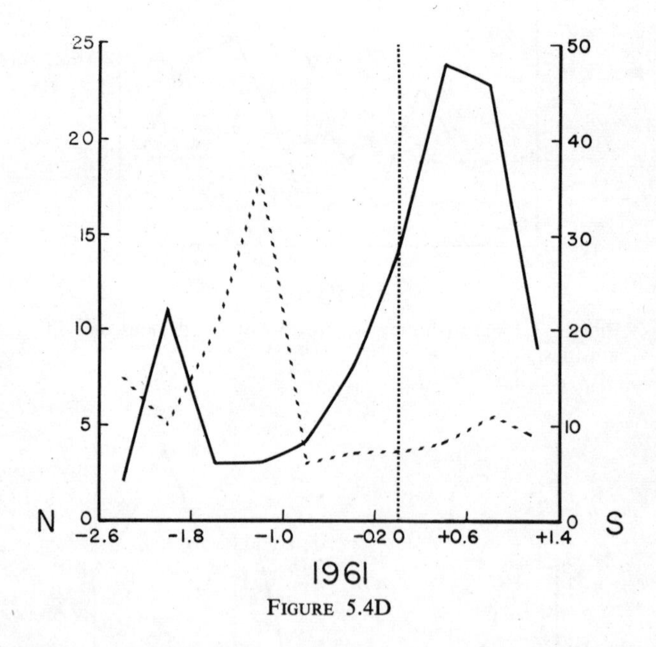

FIGURE 5.4D

South issues. We see that the development of North-South voting has been more complex. In 1947 there was some evidence for the existence of a "third party," composed of some Latins and Western Europeans. During the 1952 session the South seems largely to have controlled the Assembly, though a substantial collection of Europeans and (this time) Asians was still to be found somewhat South of center. And in 1957 this same group, augmented by most Arabs, was as large as the "revised" Northern group. But by 1961 the moderate group seems to have evaporated. Few states were prepared, at least with regard to the issues as defined in the General Assembly, to go on record as being very North or even as belonging to any very clearly defined moderate group. To be sure some Europeans are found near the middle, but numerically they are swamped by the South.

Some readers might argue that the absence of a middle group on North-South issues is partly compensated for by the near consensus at the South end of the axis. Over two thirds of the membership is to be found with scores between —.2 and +1.4. A fairly small minority can perhaps be overridden without disastrous consequences. Such a hopeful evaluation is of course belied by the composition of the "small minority": among others, France, the United Kingdom, the United States, and the Soviet bloc, all with scores greater than —1.0.

Thus on the two principal dimensions of UN voting, East-West and North-South, the evidence points to increasing bipolarity, not to the rise of a third party. On East-West issues the self-styled Afro-Asian "neutrals" in fact are generally to be found with the Soviet bloc. (Again: this is not to imply that Afro-Asians are simply following the Soviet lead; on many issues it is substantially a case of the Soviets taking up causes already dear to Afro-Asian hearts.) On those issues where the North-South alignment prevails the Afro-Asians depart very sharply from the Soviet (and European) position and take the great majority of UN members with them.

Though these features present a rather dim prospect from the vantage of our particular theoretical tower, a certain brightness would be restored if we found that even though the true neutrals were few in number, they felt rather intense about maintaining their middle position; that is, if they were active in a balancing, compromising, and mediating role. For this we must turn again to our intensity data, and combine it with the information on direction of attitudes (factor scores). We shall now look at the dashed jagged lines.

Let us return to Figure 5.3. On the whole, we do not find an intense body of neutrals on the East-West alignment. The middle powers tend to be reticent, perhaps seen but seldom heard. This is least true in 1957, when the centrists do indeed have high intensity scores. But this is probably partly due to a distortion that the uncritical counting of speeches can introduce. If a group is small, each member will have to make many speeches if the group is to hold up its end of the debate. The larger the group, the less the need (and, in fact, the more difficult it is) for every member to be heard often. So we have to bear in mind not only the number of speeches made by a country's delegation, but the number of other countries that agree with it. In doing so we can better understand what happened in 1957. The countries in the middle spoke often, but there were not too many of them. But they were not intense in 1961, when the "third party" was numerically at its low ebb. Though hardly numerous, nations near the middle of the East-West scale on the whole spoke on far fewer occasions than did those at either end.

In terms of our theory of a stable competitive system it is not necessarily a serious loss simply that the "neutrals" are not intense. We referred, after all, to hypotheses about democratic politics that suggested that a large body of apathetic neutrals helped support the system. By their own lack of interest they helped dampen the intensity of the extremists and helped prevent the lines of cleavage from becoming too clearly demarcated. But the key is in the requirement of a *large* enough body of apathetic neutrals that both sides will modify their stances in order to court it. A small group of intense, mediating neutrals may fulfill one important condition for stability. A large group of apathetic neutrals contributes in quite another but still significant way. It is when the neutrals are both few *and* apathetic that the greatest threats to stability tend to exist. And this was precisely the situation in 1961, on a voting alignment that accounted for 68 per cent of the interpretable variance in Assembly voting. Note that this discussion applies not simply to issues important in the Cold War, where there is perhaps a significant body of neutrals, but to the whole complex of issues, including both Cold War and self-determination problems, which make up the unrotated East-West factor.

Prospect and retrospect on the pattern of North-South relations are slightly less grim. As a look at Figure 5.4 will show, in at least the first three of the four years, a more or less well-defined center group is to be found with an intensity level not seriously lower than that of the extremes. Nor is this, especially in 1957, a result of the number of states to be found in the center factor-score ranges. In 1957 the center group is more intense than one would expect merely from its size, and the extremists, particularly at the South end, are less so. (This is not true for those at the very end of the South axis but is decidedly so for the aggregate in the next-to-most-extreme position.)

By 1961, however, this pattern too has shifted away toward more bipolarity, and the extremists at either end show up as the most intense. (This does not apply to the very Northern end, but that is because South Africa simply refused to participate in many of the discussions.) There is little indication of a number of center states making a serious effort as intermediaries. A very high peak of intensity does occur well to the North of center and represents to a large degree the debating activities of the United States. American UN delegates were trying to play the role of honest brokers. Yet their voting record is still very different from that of the majority of the Assembly on North-South issues, which makes one doubt whether the Americans are near enough to the middle to perform that role effectively.

Trends

Let us sum up our findings to this point about where the international political system, as reflected in the Assembly, has been and where it may be going. The most disquieting finding is perhaps the pervasiveness of the East-West conflict, so that it accounts for well over half of the voting and speech making.

It is disquieting in view also of the fact that there are a significant number of dimensions that characterize UN voting. These dimensions are uncorrelated; that is, knowing a state's allies on one dimension does not help in predicting with whom it will ally on another. Each delegation or caucusing group must maintain certain co-operative contacts with every other delegation or group, because it may expect to vote with them on at least one controversial issue or set of issues. This whole pattern of shifting vote alignments can provide a fluidity and flexibility to the system. Bargaining—the exchange of support on one issue for backing on another—is facilitated. But the more overriding East-West issues become, the more flexibility is lost. Coöperative contacts with states opposed to one on East-West questions may weaken because they are used less often. As the East-West alignment becomes more frequent relative to other dimensions, bargaining becomes more difficult.

Furthermore, we found a clear and growing bipolarity on East-West and North-South issues. Bipolarity accurately characterizes both the distribution of attitudes alone and the distribution of intense attitudes. From the evidence, true neutrals or middlemen are neither very numerous nor very intense.

Slightly more encouraging was the decline, at least within the Assembly, of the Cold War dimension. To say that strictly Cold War divisions are far less common in the UN does not necessarily indicate that they are so in the world at large. The particular requirements of UN politics undoubtedly discourage, to a growing degree, discussion of Cold War matters in the Assembly. Certainly the nonaligned states are trying to keep the Cold War out of the Assembly. Whether or not this action really contributes to a more stable world is uncertain. Maybe depriving the great powers of a propaganda forum on this subject will help reduce over-all international tension, but in a way it could actually make the settlement of Cold War disputes more difficult. The UN was, after all, designed as an arena for discussing the major issues dividing nations. Still, if the decline in Cold War attention in the Assembly truly does indicate a relaxation of the explosive Cold War conflict in the world at large, we can be heartened.

The basic East-West political pattern nevertheless remains essentially bipolar, though with some states in the middle. The factor score distributions do not provide much evidence that the major bloc leaders, especially the Soviets, are allowing themselves to be pulled very near the middle to pick up votes. Perhaps because the UN has so little power to enforce its decisions, the pressure on the great powers to play the parliamentary game is meeting with only limited success. But still there is a mediating group that attempts to mitigate the conflict. The future of politics in the UN will in large part depend upon the continuing strength of those ties that still bridge the gap between the two extremes.

CHAPTER 6

International Cross-Pressures

Influences on Voting Position

In the last two chapters we were largely concerned with the international system as a whole, and broad trends in the behavior of states in the mass. Yet an understanding of the system requires hypotheses about the behavior of particular states, or "voters." One problem is the relation between a government's constituency and the policies it pursues in the international system. In trying to affect the behavior of another state one government may appeal either directly to the other government or to the constituency beneath it. On major issues in the United Nations the American government occasionally negotiates directly with other capitals, it usually bargains with other delegations in New York, and also it often uses the General Assembly as a propaganda forum to influence world opinion. Behavior in the UN is, of course, only a part of a nation's total foreign policy. Nevertheless, UN voting, because it forces a country to take a public, recorded position on many kinds of issues, is a most valuable indicator of basic policy and pressures on policy.

According to research on American voting behavior, the individual who is not fully committed to either party is likely to be the person who is "cross-pressured." Cross-pressuring can occur in a number of ways. Originally, the description applied chiefly to sociological cross-pressures. That is, if blue-collar workers tend to vote Democratic and Protestants tend to vote Republican, then the Protestant blue-collar worker may find himself cross-pressured. Protestants will be more likely than other blue-collar workers to vote Repubican, and conversely, blue-collar workers will be more likely than other Protestants to vote Democratic. Other writers have applied the cross-pressure hypothesis more explicitly to attitude cross-pressures. Thus an individual may prefer the Democratic party but dislike President Johnson. Or he may like a candidate's stand on civil rights but disapprove of his position on foreign policy questions. Again, he will be more likely to vote against a particular candidate than will someone whose attitudes are almost entirely favorable. Furthermore, the cross-pressured voter is more likely to make up his mind late, to shift allegiances, or even not to vote at all. These are the floating voters, those who, by their relative independence, make party competition for their favor meaningful.[1]

Policy positions taken in the Assembly reflect broader national foreign policies. These policies are usually translated into resolutions, speeches, and votes in the Assembly by means of diplomatic communications from national foreign offices. When a delegate is not specifically advised, he relies on more general instructions, his own personal initiatives and obligations, and a number of national, regional, and caucusing group loyalties and attitudes. On issues that are not of material significance many of the smaller or newer states receive very few instructions. Partly because of official secrecy it is impossible to uncover systematically the specific influence of personal interpretations and national instructions on each of the issues in the Assembly. Nevertheless we can see what influences are correlated with certain kinds of voting behavior and make inferences.

Before we can discuss cross-pressures we must know what the major influences on voting behavior are. To explain UN voting positions we must examine the regional, social, economic, and political forces affecting national foreign policies. Many such variables appear relevant to Assembly voting. We know geographic location, which can be defined so as to correspond generally with the various caucusing groups in the UN. We can also use per capita G.N.P. as a measure of wealth and economic development. UN members can be classified as to the degree of competitiveness of their political systems. "Competitive" systems are democracies where two or more parties compete without government interference. "Authoritarian" regimes are here defined as those where competitive party politics is either nonexistent or rigidly controlled by the government. States satisfying neither of these conditions can be grouped in a residual category. Among such "semicompetitive" states we would include Mexico, and until the late 1950's, Pakistan and Indonesia, where a good deal of competition existed within a single party or nonelective parliament. Military alliances with the United States or with the

[1] The voting studies have elaborated and refined these points. *Cf.* Paul F. Lazarsfeld, Bernard Berelson, and Hazel Gaudet, *The People's Choice* (New York: Columbia University Press, 1944) for the origin of the concept as applied basically to sociological pressures, and A. Campbell, P. Converse, W. Miller, and Stokes, *The American Voter* (New York: John Wiley & Sons, 1960), pp. 80–88, for a careful distinction between the effects of sociological and psychological cross-pressures.

Soviet bloc can be used as measures of Cold War political alignments. We may also look at colonial status, total post-World War II foreign aid from the United States and also from the Soviet bloc, the percentage of a nation's total foreign trade with the Western Big Three (United States, Britain, and France) or with the Soviet bloc, and the racial and religious composition of UN member states. Colonial powers are here defined as those states having colonies outside of Europe at some time since 1918; ex-colonial states as those countries that were non-European colonies for any period since 1918, just before the end of World War I. The three racial and cultural variables used here are percentage Negro population, the percentage of a nation's population of European descent, and the percentage of the population that adheres to Christianity. This last is included less from any interest in religion *per se* than as an index of the influence of Western culture, especially in countries such as the Philippines or much of Latin America where the population is largely non-European in race.

All these would seem to be important influences on foreign policy-making, and most are referred to frequently in the course of UN debates. We know that groups in the Assembly feel a sense of identification and shared interests as a result of such common ties and backgrounds. We shall speak of the degree to which different socio-economic characteristics appear to polarize Assembly voting; that is, the degree to which a characteristic is concentrated at either pole of the East-West or North-South alignments. A high degree of polarization will be reflected in a high correlation between such a variable and a factor score. We cannot, of course, treat our *correlations* as *causal* relationships. They only tell us that the two are related; they do not say which causes the other, or whether both are the consequence of some third causal influence. To find causes we would have to look at many influences, to examine their effects over time, and to use a more fully developed theory. But our correlations can give us important information about cross-pressures. High correlations between socio-economic influences and policy positions indicate that cross-pressures are weak. A polarization of attitudes on North-South issues along the lines of colonial status means that colonial status contributes little cross-pressuring effect. The higher the correlations, then, the less room there is for hesitancy, for bargaining, and, according to the theory we have discussed, the greater the threat to the system's stability.

Influences on East-West and North-South Voting

Table 6.1 shows the correlation coefficients (*r*'s) as computed for voting alignments in 1961. Correlations with *Western* and with *Southern* voting are given as *negative,* and correlations of .50 and over are italicized for emphasis. We can see which regional groups and which economic, political, and cultural influences, are most closely associated with voting.

Table 6.1 **Correlations Between Regional Groups, Economic, Political, and Cultural Influences and East-West and North-South Voting, 1961** [2]

East-West	*North-South*
Regional Groups	
Soviet Bloc (*.50*)	Soviet Bloc (*.63*)
Arabs (.36)	West Europeans (.43)
Africans (.22)	Latin Americans (—.07)
Asians (.10)	Arabs (—.17)
Latin Americans (—.38)	Asians (—.23)
West Europeans (—*.58*)	Africans (—.49)
Economic Influences	
Trade with Soviet Bloc (*.56*)	Trade with Soviet Bloc (*.64*)
Soviet Bloc Aid per Capita (*.50*)	G.N.P. per Capita (.46)
Trade with Western Big 3 (—.39)	American Aid per Capita (.17)
American Aid per Capita (—.40)	Soviet Bloc Aid per Capita (.05)
G.N.P. per Capita (—.43)	Trade with Western Big 3 (—.47)
Political and Cultural Influences	
Authoritarian Regime (*.54*)	% European Descent (*.65*)
Ex-colony (*.51*)	Colonial Power (.46)
% Negro (.15)	% Christian (.43)
% European Descent (—.28)	Authoritarian Regime (.18)
Colonial Power (—.43)	Competitive System (—.00)
Competitive System (—.49)	U.S. Military Ally (—.13)
% Christian (—*.55*)	% Negro (—.41)
U.S. Military Ally (—*.78*)	Ex-colony (—*.58*)

[2] Some of these correlations appeared first in Hayward R. Alker, Jr., "Dimensions of Conflict in the General Assembly," *American Political Science Review* 58, 3 (September 1964), pp. 642–657. All appear in Hayward R. Alker, Jr. and Bruce M. Russett, *World Politics in the General Assembly* (New Haven, Conn.: Yale University Press, 1965). With regard to group memberships, "West Europeans" include United States, Canada, Australia, New Zealand, and South Africa because of their similar cultural characteristics. Outer Mongolia is considered with Soviet bloc, not Asia; Cuba, not in 1961 clearly identified as a Soviet satellite, is included only with Latin America. Turkey and Cyprus are listed with Asia. Yugoslavia, Israel, and Taiwan are not included in any regional group.

Most of the regional groupings contribute to polarizing *East-West* voting. Soviet bloc and West European memberships correlate highly with East-West factor scores; the first with East positions, of course, the second with Western positions. Arab and Latin-American memberships also correlate with East-West alignments. The Western allegiance of many former French colonies kept Africa as a whole from swinging far to the East in 1961. Asia is split down the middle. America's military allies in Asia vote West, and the "neutralists" are actually quite far East. The result has been that the Asian average is center. This is the group that, in recent years, has been most subject to East-West cross-pressures.

We would expect economic variables like trade with the Western Big Three, Soviet bloc trade, and total American and Soviet per capita military and economic aid to be highly correlated with positions on the East-West conflict. This is indeed the case, and it has remained remarkably stable through time. On the Western side trade has had as great an effect as aid. The same is true with the Soviets, with whom trade is an important means of rewarding friends or inducing friendship. Per capita G.N.P. also shows a rather high correlation with pro-Western voting positions—rich countries tend to be pro-West.

Colonial powers and ex-colonies have rather continuously opposed each other. In fact, former colonial status seems much more important in producing anti-European voting than is the racial composition of a state. In 1961 many of France's former African colonies had a habit of voting with the West, and this kept percentage Negro population from polarizing East-West voting. A common claim is that the East-West conflict is one of democracy versus authoritarianism. But actually the correlations are only moderately high; military alliances with the United States and the Soviet Union (see Soviet bloc) correlated more strongly with voting positions on this conflict. Around 60 per cent of Assembly East-West voting could be predicted just by knowing which countries were allied with the United States. Predominantly Christian countries also tend strongly to vote with the West.

Remember that the wealthier and more powerful Western and Eastern states, the West Europeans and the Soviet bloc, were identified in the preceding chapter as Northern powers. The anti-Soviet aspects of the *North-South* conflict are impressive. At the other end, Asians, Arabs, and Africans are the Southern nations, with Latin America in the middle. On North-South issues Latin, Asian, and

Arab groups are least correlated with alignment and are most susceptible to cross pressures. The Arabs, for instance, have sometimes voted with the Soviet Union on North-South issues in return for support on Palestine questions. Asian allies of the United States have increasingly taken Northern as well as Western positions (note Nationalist China); Latin Americans, in differentiating their point of view from that of the newer African states, have also been under alliance pressures to move to the West and the North. West Europeans have not always been very united in their attitudes on North-South issues, although all of them have taken more or less Northerly positions. On development, decolonialization, and disarmament issues they have often been unable to agree with the Southern nations.

In part this conflict is due to a cleavage in world politics between rich nations and poor ones; wealth has polarized North-South voting to a moderate degree. Pro-Soviet or anti-Soviet aid and trade ties correlate with North-South voting when the Soviet bloc is bearing the major brunt of anti-Northern policies. Trade with the Western Big Three has been somewhat correlated with Southern voting. In the case of trade, raw materials producers have often opposed the industrial states who buy their goods. American aid (which constitutes the bulk of Western aid) has largely been to states already wealthy by Southern standards (the Marshall Plan for Europe) or to their military allies, who have voted both West and North. For both the Soviet bloc and the West *trade* seems to distinguish Northerners from Southerners much more clearly than does *aid*.

Cultural variables and colonial status correlate quite strongly with the North-South conflict. Anti-European voting has been continuous and a more potent polarizer of Assembly voters than colonial past. Pro-Negro and non-Christian Southern polarizations also were of some weight in 1961. We see a divergence in the way Communist and American military alliances affect the North-South voting dimension. The United States has begun to take a more Southern position (chiefly in favor of strengthening the powers of the UN), and has brought some of its allies along; the Communists have always been opposed. But more important is the relative unimportance of political systems in distinguishing North from South. The democracies are rather evenly divided between North and South voting positions, though authoritarian states are fairly often North. This is true of course of the Communist bloc, and also of some authoritarian non-Communist countries like Egypt.

Cultural, economic, and anti-colonial variables have become the major Southern influences in the General Assembly. Other than the United States the most vigorous supporters of the Congo operation were the poor, non-European, and ex-colonial members of the United Nations.

To summarize: region, trade, aid, religion, political system, and former colonial status all show high correlations with the East-West dimension, as does race to a more moderate degree. The role of alliances seems to be substantial. Except in the latter case, where the correlation has been rising, these relationships have been fairly stable throughout the life of the United Nations.[3] Using the technique known as multiple regression it is possible to identify the combined effect (though it should be remembered that we still cannot prove cause) of several "independent" variables on a "dependent" variable. On the East-West conflict we can get a multiple correlation coefficient of .88 (and thus "explain" 78 per cent of the voting variation) by knowing *either* region *or* trade, aid, and military alliances.[4] With such high correlations it is clear that the role of cross-pressures in affecting East-West votes cannot be too great, except for particular groups. On the North-South dimension trade contributes strongly to the Assembly's polarization, as do race and colonial status. Aid, region, wealth, and alliances also help explain the voting, but not so much. Trade, aid, and alliances together, again using multiple regression, "explain" 70 per cent of the North-South voting variation.

Group Cohesion

Before we can go further in our discussion of cross-pressures we must have some basis for judging their apparent effect. We can perhaps best do so by looking at the voting patterns of various regional and caucusing groups and finding out which states deviate most strikingly from the voting patterns of their groups. Which individual Latin Americans vote more East, or West, or North, or South, than does the group as a whole? It is valuable to examine group deviants because, despite differences, members of various regional groups do tend to share a substantial number of socioeconomic characteristics. Also, in the previous chapter we observed a fairly high degree of unity within most of the regional groups, and much bargaining and negotiation goes on to produce intragroup agreement. Though few

[3] See Alker and Russett, *op. cit.*
[4] See Alker, *op. cit.*

Latins, for example, are as East as most Asians, it becomes essential to know which Latins are relatively East for their group.

We can construct an "index of divergence" for each group on the East-West and North-South issues in each year. Table 6.2 shows this. The index is simply the mean (or average) deviation from the average factor score of the group. A highly cohesive group will have a very low mean deviation; a disparate group a high one. We may then, to find the mavericks in each group, simply identify those states whose factor scores differ from the group average by more than the mean deviation.

Table 6.2 **Group Indices of Divergence** *

Group	*1947*	*1952*	*1957*	*1961*
	East-West			
West Europeans	.29	.17	.35	.17
Soviet Bloc	.01	.002	.02	.006
Asians	.53	.52	.60	.67
Arabs	.02	.16	.29	.22
Africans	—	—	.33	.33
Latin Americans	.51	.40	.37	.33
Average	.27	.25	.33	.29
	North-South			
West Europeans	.29	.46	.54	.62
Soviet Bloc	.12	.02	.03	.03
Asians	.32	.20	.47	.28
Arabs	.11	.21	.54	.24
Africans	—	—	.39	.25
Latin Americans	.41	.16	.51	.33
Average	.25	.21	.41	.29

* Taiwan, Israel, and Yugoslavia are listed with no group. Africans (Ethiopia and Liberia) are excluded before 1957.

Before turning to the study of individual deviant cases let us look at the divergence indices themselves. Not surprisingly the Soviet bloc turns out to be the most unified. Except for a few North-South votes in 1947, before the bloc was fully consolidated, the slight deviations can probably be accounted for by mere misunderstanding of the official position. It is notable, however, that deviation is consistently more common on North-South than on East-West issues. On several occasions when the Soviet Union made a quick tactical decision to abstain on a particular economic or colonial issue, producing something like a North-South alignment, bloc communication probably broke down.

Of the others, the Arabs are almost always among the most cohesive. Their unity has diminished somewhat since 1947 (when Palestine was so important), but it partly returned in 1961. Quite unlike the Asians, Africans, and Latin Americans, they are more unified on East-West issues than on North-South ones. The Africans, numerous enough to be considered a group only since 1957, are perhaps surprisingly united considering their division in 1961 into three caucusing subgroups (Brazzaville, Monrovia, and Casablanca). The Asians, always sharply split on East-West issues, have become more so. Their unity on North-South issues is significantly greater but has fluctuated rather widely. Latin America too has been rather sharply divided, but has consistently become more unified over the years, especially on East-West colonial attitudes. If one were to delete Cuba from the Latin-American group in 1961 the increased cohesion would be even greater. Finally, the West Europeans, despite Austria, Ireland, and the Scandinavian neutrals, have always been rather highly unified on East-West issues, though their unity on North-South matters is rapidly disappearing.

One feature of these patterns is the tendency for a group to be more unified the nearer it is to an extreme. The Latins have, as a group, been "moving" West since 1952. Similarly the West Europeans have been shifted slightly West and become more unified. A majority of the Asians has increasingly parted company with the Western-oriented states of Turkey, Japan, the Philippines, Thailand, and Iran. These five states together have become more unified as they moved West, and the remaining Asians are increasingly united without them (though the average factor score for the non-Western Asians has not changed significantly). On the North-South dimension the Latins were more unified in 1952, when they were farthest South. The Arabs were as a group farthest South in 1947 and in close agreement; in 1957, when the group average was almost precisely in the middle of the North-South axis, Arab voting unity reached its lowest ebb. To some extent extremeness (and unity) is associated with the importance of an issue to a group. Palestine was a key North-South issue in 1947, but was relatively unimportant a decade later.

There are, of course, exceptions. The Arabs have, as a group, shifted slightly to the East and have lost unity. Asian states are basically Southern; no consistent relation between unity and group position on the North-South dimension emerges. The Old Europeans have become more deeply divided on North-South issues as the group average has become more North; even here, however, a substantial part of the apparent Northern shift is due not to movement of the group as a whole but to the increasing isolation of France, South Africa, and Portugal.

Thus, with exceptions, there seems to be a general tendency for group cohesion to be associated with extremeness. Given the growing polarization of the Assembly discussed in the previous chapter this would suggest that the power of cross-pressures to mitigate conflict *between* regional groups has declined. This conclusion—the lessening power of cross-pressures to mitigate conflict between states in *different* regional groups—is supported by the lower average divergence index in 1961 than in 1957. Still, that index remained slightly higher in 1961 than in 1947 or 1952.

Explaining Deviations

We can now look in detail at deviating states and try to discover what influences are associated with departure from the average position of a group of states. In a sense we are faced with a huge variety of possible explanatory influences, each of which explains some but hardly all of the voting patterns.

For example, we may try to explain deviation by patterns of trade and aid. We found a very high over-all correlation between these economic variables and East-West voting. They also work very well as explanations of differences *within* groups. The three most Western African states in 1961 were Cameroons, Dahomey, and the Malagasy Republic; they ranked fifth, second, and fourth, respectively, in per capita economic aid received from France. Among Arabs, Jordan, Lebanon, and Tunisia were second, third, and fourth (behind Libya) in per capita aid from the Western Big Three; they were the three most pro-Western states in voting. Turkey, Japan, Thailand, and the Philippines were West of the Asian group by more than a mean deviation. Respectively they ranked second, sixth, seventh, and third as aid recipients among the sixteen Asian UN members.[5]

These pro-Western states received aid exclusively, or virtually so,

[5] This excludes Taiwan, which is not a member of the Afro-Asian caucusing group. But its behavior underlines the point—it ranked higher both in Westernness and in aid than any member of the group.

from the West. The most Eastern states in each of these groups always received aid from both sides. The five Asians who were East of the group average by more than a mean deviation—Indonesia, Afghanistan, Nepal, India, and Cambodia—all were in the top six Sino-Soviet aid recipients in Asia. Iraq and Egypt led the Arabs in Eastern voting and trailed only Syria on aid. Guinea, Ghana, Mali, Somalia, and Ethiopia led the Africans in both departments. Total Sino-Soviet bloc aid to these 12 countries was about $25 per capita at the time the 16th General Assembly met in 1961. Every one of these states also received aid from the Western Big Three, though it averaged only about half that from Communist countries.

As we cautioned earlier it is not easy to say who is controlling whom in this kind of relationship. We cannot say whether one major bloc principally aids proven friends or whether it to some degree actually buys votes. One would normally expect some combination of the two to operate with different force in each case. Probably it is really a mutually reinforcing process.

But however powerful economic bonds may be as explanations of voting behavior they leave much unaccounted for. The prime example is Latin America. Every Latin state has received aid from the United States—less aid than has been sent to Europe but more, on a per capita basis, than has gone to most Afro-Asians. Correspondingly the Latins have been, as a group, more Eastern than Europe but more Western than Afro-Asia. But neither trade with the United States nor economic aid is at all correlated with deviations *within* the Latin-American group. Those whose economies are most closely bound to the United States are *not* its closest allies in the Assembly.

Though trade with the United States does not help to explain Latin-American voting, trade within the regional group does. We shall work with a crude but simple and objective measure of economic interdependence. In 1954 all countries of the world exported a total of $77 billion of goods, of which about 12 per cent went to Latin America. Paraguay, however, sent a third of its total exports to Latin-American states, a figure well above the world average. This difference between actual and "world average" is, in essence, our measure. We then can construct a simple table with cells for countries who export below the world average to their own regional groups and those whose exports are equal to or above the world average. In addition one can separate those countries whose factor scores are equal to or less than one mean deviation from the group average score, and those whose factor scores are farther, either negatively or positively, than one mean deviation away. Two such tables, one for East-West and one for North-South, follow (Table 6.3). They allow us to see whether a high level of trade with one's regional group is associated with a political position similar to the group. The data are for all four years; thus a country that has been in the UN since 1947 was counted four times, whereas the newest members were counted only in 1961.

Table 6.3 **Voting Cohesion and Economic Integration with the Group**

East-West Factor Scores

Exports to Group	≤ 1 Mean Deviation from Group Average	> 1 Mean Deviation from Group Average	Total
≥ World Average	92	55	147
< World Average	33	35	68
Total	125	90	215

North-South Factor Scores

Exports to Group	≤ 1 Mean Deviation from Group Average	> 1 Mean Deviation from Group Average	Total
≥ World Average	87	60	147
< World Average	37	31	68
Total	124	91	215

For the East-West dimension, then, there is a clear association between economic integration and voting cohesion. Countries that trade heavily with their regional groups are more likely to vote with the group.[6] Trade integration is a particularly good predictor of Latin-American voting on East-West issues, which was not related to trade with the United States. Eleven Latin states sent a smaller proportion of their exports to other Latins than did the world as a whole. Over the four years analyzed, 30 states (counting most twice or more) had factor scores that differed from the group average by more than a mean deviation. In 22 of these 30 instances the divergent state was one that was not closely integrated with the group.

Even so, trade hardly explains everything. A particularly striking exception is Lebanon. Thanks largely to its geographic position and

[6] The association between trade and voting with the group on North-South issues is much weaker than on East-West issues. The former are surely much less important to most states than the major Cold War and colonialism issues that make up the East-West dimension; thus there may be much less pressure to maintain group unity.

entrepôt trade Lebanon is more closely integrated, in an economic sense, with her regional group than is any other state with its own group. Yet in voting Lebanon is consistently one of the most Western, and one of the most Southern, of the Arab nations.

At this point one clearly must bring in other cultural, political, and economic variables as explanations. Close examination of the deviants suggests numerous complementary hypotheses. Approximately half of Lebanon's population is Christian, a Western characteristic. Excepting only Israel and the oil shiekdoms, Lebanon's per capita income is the highest in the Middle East. It has a free enterprise economy, and its political system is by far the most democratic of any Arab country. Lebanon is thus heavily pulled toward the West by a number of cross-pressures. Perhaps its Western voting, despite its commercial relations with other Arabs, can be traced not to any one of these influences but to their unique combination.

In 1961 the four most Western Asians were, in order, Turkey, Japan, the Philippines, and Thailand. All are military allies of the United States. All have free enterprise economies. The first three are democracies. Turkey has always been a European power as well as an Asian one; part of Turkey is in Europe; the Turks are members of NATO. Japan has been more deeply affected by Western industrial curture than perhaps any other Asian state. The Philippines are predominantly Christian, with English the major language. Turkey, the Philippines, and especially Japan are, by Asian standards, economically well off.

Again it is difficult to single out any particular influence. Alliance may be a major one, but Iran and Pakistan, two other Western allies, are only slightly to the West of the Asian center. A few other Asian states are as rich as at least Turkey and the Philippines. It would appear that the combination of Western influences, rather than any single one, is largely responsible. The same kind of explanation would apply to Turkey and Japan who, with Afghanistan (whose voting closely parallels the Soviet Union's), were the most Northern Asians.

Similarly one can explain deviations in negative terms; that is, the absence of economic and social characteristics that are common to other members of the regional group. Haiti is, in almost every respect, the least Western of the Latin-American states. Its per capita income is as low as any in the hemisphere. Its population is black, it does not share the Iberian culture of the rest of the region, and its cultural ties with France are at best tenuous. Four fifths of the people speak a Creole patois unintelligible to a Frenchman. Even nominally its Roman Catholic population is proportionately the smallest of the Latin states (70 per cent), and for many their Catholicism is heavily spiked with Voodoo. Many commentators have called it just another underdeveloped African country. Thus it is no surprise to find Haiti at the Easternmost edge of the Latin-American voting group. Among Old Europeans the Easternmost states are usually either poor (Greece, Portugal in 1961) or those who, as neutrals, are not tied in with Western security arrangements.

One of the most striking features of the North-South pattern is the difficulty encountered in explaining within-group variations. Intragroup trade, which was used rather successfully as a partial explanation of East-West voting, was not much help on the North-South dimension. Neither do most of the variables that earlier were so powerful in identifying North-South characteristics *in the Assembly as a whole* help much. European race, economic development, alliance, Christian religion, trade and aid from the West; *within groups* all are only very slightly correlated with North voting, and sometimes even negatively within the Latin, or Asian, or Arab, or African caucusing groups.

Only two variables work at all well. One is colonial status, which discriminates powerfully within the Old European and Asian groups. All the Old European states (nine) who were North of the group average in 1961 were colonial powers; only two colonial nations—Italy and the Netherlands—were to be found South of the group average. Among the Asians, four of the five states that were not once colonies—Japan, Nepal, Thailand, and Turkey—were North of their group, and two of those, Japan and Turkey, were themselves former colonial powers. Of the noncolonies, only Iran was more Southern than the group average. The other variable that discriminates well is aid from the Soviet bloc, which is almost as good a "predictor" of Northern voting as it is for Eastern alignment. In the Arab group the three highest per capita aid recipients—Syria, Egypt, and Iraq—were in 1961 the fifth, fourth, and second most Northern states. Similarly, Afghanistan was most Northern, Cambodia was fifth, and Indonesia was fourth in Asia. And in Africa the four chief recipients of Soviet aid all ranked in the top six of Northern-voting states.

The failure to find higher socioeconomic correlations with voting on North-South issues is puzzling and, at the same time rather disturbing. It is disturbing because of the role that cross-pressures supposedly play in mitigating conflict. From our data it would appear that the common cross-cutting solidarities do not have much effect within groups. Variables such as race and development are important influences on the over-all pattern but not within the blocs. This suggests that the North-South conflict may contain the seeds of an especially bitter quarrel, one that in the long run might not be restrained by world-wide ties even as much as the East-West struggle is now restrained.

Seeking a Buffer

We began these three chapters with the idea that if long-term rivalry between East and West was indeed in prospect, the stability of the system would depend upon the existence of a group or groups who were not fully aligned with either side. This group or groups might take the form of an active, intense, and cohesive neutral body, or it might be simply a large number of states who, though neither very cohesive nor very intense about being neutral, simply were numerous enough, and flexible enough, always to constitute a body of floating voters, not very involved in the central East-West controversies, chiefly interested in more parochial concerns, and ready to bargain with both East and West to further their own ends. Or finally, it might take the somewhat different form of two or more major alignments, or dimensions, of voting behavior. Each of these alignments would occur often, and they would be uncorrelated—the position of a state on one alignment would not be a good predictor of its position on another alignment. If this occurred it would not be so important whether or not there was a substantial middle on either alignment, because the existence of two or more dimensions would mean, by definition, that the whole international system was not polarized and that there would likely be room for bargaining and log-rolling.

In the latter sense our findings have not been encouraging. Various separate issues have increasingly become regarded as East-West issues, and the voting alignments on Cold War and colonial issues have become increasingly similar. All interests hardly coincide on these issues, and it is not always easy to tell who is leading whom; nevertheless the alignments are similar and, to an ever greater extent, have come to dominate the Assembly. North-South questions, defined by a separate and distinct voting alignment, are becoming rarer. It is true that some issues that do not load heavily on the East-West factor—such as the Congo votes—were clearly major issues and of great importance for the future of the organization. To some degree this kind of quality may make up for what is lacking in quantity. But the hard facts of the voting patterns give little cause for more than a very modest optimism.

If cross-cutting voting dimensions are not to provide the fluidity necessary to our desired system we must look for a middle group, either numerous or intense, on East-West issues. But there was little sign of a middle group growing either in number or intensity. A hope that cross-pressures within a regional or caucusing group might force it to a middle position was, with one significant exception, not borne out. In their voting, at least, the Scandinavians were never terribly nearer the center than other Old Europeans; they certainly have not been recently. The Latins have tended to become more cohesive as they have moved nearer the extreme. The Arabs are quite East and quite unified.

The Asians are far from cohesive and are, on the average, not too near the Eastern pole. This is true because of the severe cross-pressures to which a number of pro-Western Asian nations are subject. The effect of these cross-pressures, however, has not been to modify the position of Asians as a whole. On the contrary it has been to create an ever-widening gulf between the quite Eastern majority and a Western-leaning minority. Instead of bringing all Asians toward a less extreme position, the effect of the Western ties of some (and conversely, the ties of others with the Soviets) has been to diminish the compromising and mediating effects of their common Asian bonds.

Possibly the chief hope of a nonpolarized Assembly lies with its largest but weakest grouping: the non-Arab Africans. The African group was reasonably cohesive in 1961. Its divergence index was .33, far better than the Asians (.67) and not worse than the newly coalescing Latins (.33). It is particularly striking to find such high agreement among states in the center. Most sub-Saharan states were able, within limits, to concur on a middle-of-the-road policy on East-West questions. The Latins, by contrast, achieved relative consensus only when a number of former "centrists" shifted West to join the main body of the group. And finally, African agreement is impressive when one remembers that most members of the African group also belonged to a separate caucusing subgroup.[7] Even these subgroups apparently did not divide African loyalties *too* seriously. Too much cohesion, of course, could be as dangerous to the system as too little. The virtue of a group of "balancers" is that they form a floating vote,

[7] These subgroups have since been disbanded.

aligning now with one side, then with another, and often being sufficently divided for some members of the group to be picked off by either side. A too uniform cohesion and rigid noncommitment to either side would deprive the group of its stabilizing value. It must, after all, be able to hold out the prospect of availability to those who seek its support.

Africa provides a perfect example of what it means to be cross-pressured, yet at the same time somewhat remote from the great struggle. Economically the states south of the Sahara are almost uniquely vulnerable. Most of them remain in the franc or sterling monetary zones, and are closely bound to their former metropolitan territories. It is not unusual for an African state to carry on two thirds or more of its trade with the United States-Britain-France; half did so in 1960 or 1961. Such firm ties of current trade mean that virtually all of their capital equipment was made by one of these three great Western industrial powers; thus replacement parts too must come from the West. At the same time a number are trying, with some success, to establish aid and trade relations with the Communist countries. By mid-1962 Guinea, Ghana, Somalia, Mali, Ethiopia, and Senegal all had received Sino-Soviet bloc aid. And in one crucial economic variable—per capita income—they are very non-Western.

Culturally too, they are cross-pressured. Thanks to the success of Western missionaries in formerly pagan lands, Christians are fairly numerous throughout Africa, and actually make up a majority of the population in quite a few states. Only in the Philippines, of Asian states, has Christianity had such a Westernizing impact at least in numerical terms. But at the same time a major Eastern religion, Islam, is also strong in many African states, and it too is the majority religion in several. Finally, many areas of Africa have resisted both of these influences. And of course in color they are non-Western without necessarily feeling more than a negative sort of bond with Asians.

Nor are most of the new African elites irrevocably bound to the political systems of either camp. Most were trained in Western or Western-run schools—unlike Asia, Africa had little in the way of local resources for education. Yet few members of these elites are deeply committed to democracy as it is understood in Europe or the Commonwealth. Few too, despite strong Marxist influences, are orthodox Communists. They may mouth ideologies either of state ownership or of private enterprise, but in many cases this ideology represents less a basic emotional or intellectual commitment than a response to foreign or domestic pressures. The Liberian government, with its dependence on Firestone Rubber, talks about free enterprise; the Guineans, less rich in foreign investments, choose otherwise.

In competing for the allegiance of African "voters," then, the West has some important strengths: religion, the Western training of most elites, the cultural residue of colonialism, and current economic ties of trade and aid. The East too has its influences: Islam, some economic ties, and color. But neither West nor East has made a deep impression on Africa. Perhaps most influential in the end will be the uniquely African characteristics referred to by Africans themselves as "negritude." Already there are indications, such as the disbanding of the separate Monrovia, Casablanca, and Brazzaville groups, that African common interests may count for more in the international arena than the interests that divide the continent. This is *not* to imply that African political unity, in the sense of a common government, is around the corner. Such a prediction would require a totally different study. It does imply that as international actors a sort of African parochialism may tend to keep the states relatively cohesive as a voting bloc.[8]

Thus prospects may be for an Africa that is apathetic toward many aspects of world conflict, and able to maintain a middle and fairly unified position between the two camps. Africa is not a power in the larger world of international politics; it is too weak. But in the peculiarly distorted yet important arena of the UN it may yet be a moderating force. This cannot happen until all the "African self-determination" problems—South Africa, Southern Rhodesia, the Portuguese territories like Angola—leave the center stage. While colonialism remains in its most obvious political form, Africans will have extreme opinions keenly felt. And the elimination of colonialism, when it comes, may do so with such racial violence as to deepen yet further the East-West gulf and throw the Africans irrevocably away from the middle.

If this outcome can be avoided the Africans may become that group of apathetics, wooed but never won, that can mitigate conflict and provide the basis for a stable order. Essentially, the question is what will be the most prominent dimension of future UN sessions.

[8] Thomas Hovet, in *Africa in the United Nations* (Evanston, Ill.: Northwestern University Press, 1963), presents convincing evidence of parochialism and indifference to Cold War problems. Most striking is his report (p. 219) that a delegate of one of the older African states, an important official in his own government and an experienced representative on the Main Committee concerned with Korea, did not know that the Korean peninsula is divided into two states, North and South.

If it should be the Cold War, Africa would seem uniquely suited to play the center position. But over most of the life of the UN the trend has been toward a decline in the prominence of Cold War issues, and a rise in that of self-determination questions. Some observers believe that colonialism too is a dying issue in the world organization, as the last territories achieve independence. Yet announcement of the birth of the "post-colonial world" may be premature. Still another candidate for prominence in the coming years may be the set of issues involving rich-poor relations. If either self-determination or rich-poor questions predominate, the Africans almost certainly will be far from the middle. In such a case the role of neutral balancer will fall to countries elsewhere in the non-European world. Asians, and perhaps especially Latin Americans, may yet find themselves with the keys to peace.[9]

[9] Some of the conclusions of this chapter and the preceding one would be modified by an examination of other alignments and other influences. For a more complete study see Alker and Russett, *op. cit.*

CHAPTER 7

Trends in World Inequality

Revolutions and Inequality

Most people believe that revolutions arise as a reaction to great inequalities of wealth or income. Perhaps so, but all situations of great inequality are by no means equally likely to end in revolution. Many instances of the grossest repression continue for decades or even centuries without serious revolt; other cases of much milder inequity may result in violent upheaval and bloody revenge upon the former dominant group. The peculiar mixture of circumstances that produce revolution is still only imperfectly understood; undoubtedly it varies under different historical conditions and different incentives to revolt. Nevertheless certain common elements do seem always to be present:

1. Inequality in the distribution of something that is widely valued, like money, farm land, political power, or even respect.
2. The possibility of comparison. Those who are poor must have some means of knowing that others live very much better; they must see that others are better off and have some basis, however distorted, of recognizing their own poverty.
3. Some means of communicating with others who feel themselves deprived, so as to make joint action possible.
4. Some possibility of success, at least in the minds of the potential revolutionaries. No matter how downtrodden, men will seldom revolt in large numbers unless they see a reasonably good chance to succeed. Now the meaning of "reasonably good" may vary with the circumstances, and desperate, badly oppressed men will certainly take greater chances than men who are fairly well off. Also, potential revolutionaries seldom can evaluate their chances with perfect accuracy. They are human, fallible, and may take chances that objectively would not be justified.

As citizens of the richest country on earth, where even ordinary people have a standard of living which surpasses that of all but a fraction of the world's population, Americans cannot ignore the problem of inequality and its implications for world politics. People in underdeveloped countries are becoming increasingly aware of their poverty; they know that by comparison with the nations of Europe and North America they are poor, and they think that somehow they can find the means to raise their living standards. The questions of crucial importance to world peace are: to what extent will the improvement in these countries' economic conditions keep pace with increasing demands, "the revolution of rising expectations," and, in cases of shortfall, what kinds of solutions are the world's poor likely to seek?

Because much of the world is poor while parts of it are rich does not mean that the rich necessarily planned it that way in any kind of greedy or diabolical plot. Few of us, who are the world's privileged, can honestly say that we have any major control over the system, that we deliberately oppress anyone, or that if we individually tried to change the world's distribution of income in the direction of greater equality we could actually succeed. As far as we are concerned there simply *are* rich and poor; "the poor are with you always." We (or our fathers) have worked hard for what we have, and we did not steal it (usually); poor people, in our own country as elsewhere, are poor because they lack the skills, the education, the capital, or the opportunities to better themselves. Sometimes we say too that poor people in our country are poor because they lack the intelligence or the ambition to improve their status. To whatever degree that is true in America, however, there is no reason to believe that Americans are as a nation more intelligent than Chinese, or even more ambitious—providing that you present the average Chinese with an opportunity where ambition will do him some good.

Marxists have tried to explain world inequalities in terms of their theory of how capitalism operates. According to the Communists, capitalists in industrial countries are faced with an ever declining rate of profit. Many firms fail, and the remainder become larger and more monopolistic. Capitalists become fewer, the proletariat becomes larger, and the downfall of the capitalist system is ever more imminent. The capitalists, says Lenin, try to postpone their doom by exporting capital. They find both markets and labor in the backward countries of the world, and persuade their own governments to take over political control of them as colonies. The people in these countries are brought under the capitalist system and impoverished; the capitalists of the advanced countries gain a respite, and for a time, the workers in the imperialist states may find their condition improving. Capitalists—or, more precisely the capitalist system, for individual capitalists are merely driven by economic forces and are not personally evil—are thus to blame for the impoverishment of the underdeveloped states, and only by the overthrow of capitalism will they escape poverty.

Now this argument is sometimes persuasive to inhabitants of poor countries, but it ignores some important if inconvenient facts. The acquisition of colonies by America and Britain in the late nineteenth century was not primarily the result of capitalists' demands for markets; on the contrary, many industrialists opposed imperialism for fear that it might result in war that would be bad for business. Since the end of World War II almost all of the former colonies have achieved political independence, but few of them are developing more rapidly as independent states than they did as colonial territories. In fact, many, like the Congo (Leopoldville), Burma, Indonesia, and Algeria, have stagnated under independence. Marxists might maintain that though politically sovereign in theory they are stili in economic bondage to the foreign capitalists who control their import and export trade. But actually there is little evidence that a colonial past makes much difference in the rate or level of development in African and Asian countries. Thailand, though long independent, is not notably more wealthy than her neighbors. Afghanistan and Ethiopia were never colonies (except for about five years for Ethiopia), nor were they ever seriously penetrated by Western capitalism. They also are notably neither poorer nor richer than neighboring states that were colonies. It is true that in many instances the colonial powers failed to develop their colonies other than to the degree that was necessary to build raw material exporting industries and to tighten political control. But neglect of development is not the same as active impoverishment, for which there is little evidence.

Western states therefore cannot fairly be blamed, as villains, for the low living standards of most of the world. The wealth of the West is absolutely unique in world history. Medieval Europe was probably not much better off than modern Southeast Asia or the Middle East. In the Renaissance and, much more substantially in the Industrial Revolution, Western Europe embarked on a period of rapid development without precedent, a process whose causes we still do not thoroughly understand. But the result of Europe's development has been to create an enormous gap between the Western industrial nations and Asia, Africa, and Latin America. Unless this gap begins fairly rapidly to narrow, part of the necessary foundation for a revolutionary situation will have been laid.

The Distribution of World Welfare

In fact, the gap has been narrowing very slightly, despite popular opinion to the contrary. It has been a common expression that "the rich get richer and the poor get poorer" (or, in one variant, "the poor get children"). This certainly was true during the nineteenth and early twentieth centuries, when rapid economic development continued at a much faster pace in the West than in Africa and Asia—in many parts of the East per capita income hardly grew at all.[1] But by the middle of this century the situation had begun to change. Table 7.1 presents estimates of G.N.P. per capita for 30 important countries in 1950; it also presents projections for G.N.P. per capita in 1975.

How do we go about making projections? One method would involve true *prediction*; making estimates based upon a detailed knowledge of the situation in each country and of the conditions that will affect economic growth in coming years. Now obviously this kind of demand is totally unreasonable. The prospects for economic growth depend upon the unemployment situation, on political policies, on international developments, and on a host of other factors that cannot be predicted with any degree of accuracy. We cannot reasonably say even who will win the next Presidential election, let alone what his policies will be and what effects they will have. (Considering the importance economic growth has played as an issue in recent campaigns we surely do think political acts really affect it.)

Another method, which does not involve one in making impossible judgments about the consequences of a million and one factors, is to compute the rates of change in something like G.N.P. over a given past time and project these same rates into the future. Assume, in other words, that the situation in the future will change at the same rate as in the past. Such a procedure is only one of *projection,* not *prediction*. It says what would happen *if* the rates remained unchanged, but does not predict that they *will* be unchanged. It is therefore a method of "persistence forecasting." By its very nature this method of course cannot identify any change in trends, and it is therefore less useful the longer the projection one attempts. Here, however, we shall attempt projections only for a moderate time span, to 1975. We shall project from around 1960, using the rates that applied in the decade 1950 to 1960. In the tables you will find only

[1] See Simon Kuznets, "Regional Economic Trends and Levels of Living," in Phillip Hauser (ed.), *Population and World Politics* (New York: The Free Press, 1958), pp. 79–118.

the figures for 1950 and 1975, but they are based on actual developments up to about 1960. By this procedure we see what the world would look like in 1975 *if* past trends continued. Because some past trends cannot or will not continue, some of our projections will look peculiar, but they can nevertheless assist us in identifying problem areas and trends of particular consequence.

Table 7.1 G.N.P. per Capita *

1950		*1975*	
United States	$2300	United States	$3550
Canada	1750	West Germany	2900
Britain	1200	Canada	2600
Belgium	1000	Czechoslovakia	1950
France	750	Belgium	1875
Netherlands	675	Britain	1800
West Germany	600	France	1750
Argentina	500	U.S.S.R.	1625
Venezuela	480	Netherlands	1475
Czechoslovakia	450	Venezuela	1400
U.S.S.R.	400	Italy	1330
Italy	350	Poland	1300
Chile	340	Japan	1140
Poland	320	Yugoslavia	925
Spain	290	Spain	700
Brazil	235	Brazil	500
Mexico	225	Chile	480
Colombia	220	Argentina	455
Turkey	200	Mexico	395
Japan	190	Colombia	390
Philippines	185	Philippines	335
Yugoslavia	165	Turkey	305
Egypt	135	Egypt	285
Indonesia	120	China	190
Thailand	85	Indonesia	170
Nigeria	70	Thailand	130
Pakistan	70	Burma	115
India	70	Nigeria	95
China	50	India	85
Burma	45	Pakistan	75

* In this table and those following the source of the data and the rates of change is Bruce M. Russett *et al.*, *World Handbook of Political and Social Indicators* (New Haven, Conn.: Yale University Press, 1964). In a few cases change rates are estimated. All G.N.P. figures are in 1957 dollars.

We find some rather startling changes between the situation of 1950 and that projected for 1975. The United States will, if these projections are correct, remain the richest country in the world, but it will be followed fairly closely by West Germany. If they are even approximately accurate, by 1975 the Soviet Union and Eastern Europe will have a per capita product not far short of the projected average for much of Western Europe, and very far above the 1950 Western European average. Communist China will also have made very significant gains, and Japan's per capita G.N.P. will be well above that of Europe in 1950. Most of Latin America (except for stagnating Argentina) will show real but modest gains (Venezuela, however, shows the effects of a rather high growth rate). But major segments of the non-Communist underdeveloped world—India, Pakistan, and Indonesia, for example—are likely to grow only very slowly in per capita G.N.P.

Actually, of course, there is no reason to believe that these projections will be borne out just as they appear here. It seems reasonable, for example, to expect the growth rate for several European countries to be slower in the 1960's than it was in the previous decade, as postwar recovery is completed and the early stimulation of the Common Market wears off. Probably also the Communist countries will not do quite so well as would appear. Much of the success of Soviet-type economics in achieving rapid industrialization is due to their ability, through totalitarian political controls, to maintain a higher level of investment and a lower level of consumption than their people would freely choose if given the opportunity. But to some degree they are assisted by the ability to adopt or adapt technological advances that are developed in other more advanced countries.[2] The more economically developed the Communist countries themselves become, the harder it is to continue development without a massive and expensive scientific base. Though the Russians have built just such a base their efforts seem unlikely to compensate them entirely for their losses in ability to borrow technology. Declines in East and West European growth rates were actually in evidence in the early 1960's, and they are not fully reflected in our projections, nor is the very serious floundering of Communist China's "great leap forward" in the late 1950's and early 1960's. But they are not likely to be so

[2] Much of the Soviet Union's technology is fully as advanced as that in the West, but important segments, especially agriculture and consumer goods production, could still benefit enormously from the use of European or American methods.

wrong as to change the general picture seriously and do reflect true developments up to 1960.

For some of the same reasons that we mentioned in Chapter 1 with respect to total G.N.P. as a measure of power, G.N.P. per capita tends to exaggerate differences in welfare. Partly this is the result of differences in prices in underdeveloped and industrialized countries. Another difficulty might be labeled "costs of civilization." A substantial part of an industrialized country's G.N.P. is devoted not directly to the comfort of the population but to making the high level of production and industrialization possible. Urbanization brings its own special costs in terms of crowding, air and water pollution, need for mass transit facilities, and so on. A city worker earning the same wage as a rural laborer probably has a lower standard of living—unless he attaches significant value to the real cultural or other advantages of city life. Another complexity is added by climate. A Mediterranean dweller has free a climate that a Scandinavian can provide only indoors, and only at great expense. For these reasons G.N.P. per capita is a better measure of *production* than of *welfare*, and we can never say with confidence that people in a country that has twice the per capita G.N.P. of another have twice as high a standard of living. But we can feel reasonably confident about our rankings, and about relative changes in the over-all pattern of inequality in distribution.

One aspect of welfare is health, the access to medical care. Table 7.2 shows the number of inhabitants per hospital bed in most of the same 30 countries that appeared in the previous table, again with data for 1950 and projections, based on 1950–1960 rates of change, to 1975. As with G.N.P. as a measure of living standards, this index has its disadvantages, especially because it cannot indicate the quality of hospital care. Nevertheless where we have data it correlates highly with other indices like life expectancy and infant mortality rates, and so it seems a reasonable rough indicator.[3]

All of the poor countries represented in Table 7.2 appear to be catching up in health conditions (though we have no data for several important underdeveloped countries). Also some nations in the middle-income ranges, like Venezuela and Eastern Europe, show definite improvement. A few wealthy countries, however, threaten

[3] For a more detailed discussion of the uses and limitations of the indices employed in this chapter see Bruce M. Russett *et al., World Handbook of Political and Social Indicators* (New Haven, Conn.: Yale University Press, 1964).

Table 7.2 Inhabitants per Hospital Bed

1950		*1975*	
Britain	90	Italy	70
Canada	90	Japan	70
France	90	Netherlands	70
West Germany	90	U.S.S.R.	70
United States	100	Czechoslovakia	75
Czechoslovakia	120	Canada	80
Belgium	140	Belgium	110
Italy	140	Yugoslavia	110
Argentina	160	Poland	120
Poland	170	West Germany	130
U.S.S.R.	170	Britain	140
Netherlands	190	United States	140
Japan	200	Argentina	160
Chile	210	Venezuela	200
Yugoslavia	320	Philippines	210
Venezuela	330	Brazil	220
Brazil	340	Turkey	220
Colombia	380	France	240
Egypt	540	Colombia	260
Turkey	1000	Chile	370
Philippines	1500	Thailand	380
Indonesia	1600	Egypt	400
Burma	2000	Burma	770
Thailand	2300	Indonesia	920
India	2500	Nigeria	1400
Nigeria	2700	India	1600
China	?	China	?
Mexico	?	Mexico	?
Pakistan	?	Pakistan	?
Spain	?	Spain	?

to fall behind. Perhaps one of the most striking facts about this table is the fact that even in 1950 the United States was not at the top of the list, and has since fallen. Possibly the quality of American medical care is good enough to compensate for its higher inhabitant per hospital bed ratio, but it does happen that the United States also trails Britain in life expectancy and infant mortality rate. Overall, our general impression is that of an improvement in the status of the most deprived people and perhaps therefore a decrease in one of the elements of a revolutionary situation. This is unlike the distribution of G.N.P. per capita, where on the whole it was the middle-income countries that showed the greatest improvement.

Access to Communications

Now that we have some general indication of trends in living standards and health conditions, we can look at the second element in our evaluation of the potential for violent conflict—trends in access to means of communication.

Table 7.3 **Percentage of Adults Literate**

1950		*1975*	
Belgium	99	Belgium	99
Canada	99	Britain	99
Netherlands	99	Canada	99
West Germany	99	Czechoslovakia	99
Czechoslovakia	98	France	99
Britain	98	Italy	99
United States	97	Japan	99
France	96	Netherlands	99
Japan	95	Philippines	99
Italy	88	Poland	99
Poland	88	United States	99
Argentina	87	U.S.S.R.	99
U.S.S.R.	80	West Germany	99
Chile	79	Spain	98
Spain	79	Argentina	95
Yugoslavia	69	Chile	92
Philippines	64	Yugoslavia	88
Colombia	62	Thailand	87
Thailand	56	Venezuela	77
Venezuela	52	Colombia	73
Mexico	50	Mexico	66
Brazil	49	China	65
Burma	48	Brazil	61
China	48	Turkey	59
Turkey	34	Burma	55
Egypt	21	Egypt	31
India	19	Indonesia	30
Indonesia	18	India	26
Pakistan	13	Pakistan	20
Nigeria	10	Nigeria	15

The table shows the proportion of adults who are literate in each of the 30 countries. For any country 99 per cent literacy represents a virtual ceiling beyond which it is impossible to go. We see that even in 1950 the developed nations were already at the level of virtually complete literacy, and could do little more in promoting this basic skill. But by 1975 a number of underdeveloped or semideveloped countries will attain literacy rates of over 90 per cent, if recent trends continue. In fact, almost two fifths of the world's population will live in such countries. Even Communist China and most Latin American countries are likely to be well over half literate. Now literacy of course does not imply the possession of detailed knowledge or a high level of education or technical skill such as would enable a person to perform a complex job in a modern industrial society. But it is almost certainly a prerequisite for much economic development. It also implies a certain access to information (and sometimes misinformation) about the world outside one's own limited locality. It can provide a benchmark for comparing one's immediate status with that of others, and thus provides the potential for the "revolution of rising expectations." It also provides the basis for mass communication—a basis that, although surely not ominous in itself, nevertheless makes a revolutionary situation possible.

We can also look at the world distribution of another important element of mass communications—access to radios. Table 7.4 shows radios per 1000 inhabitants in the same countries as in the previous table (except for China, for which we have no data).

Table 7.4 **Radios per 1000 Inhabitants**

1950		*1975*	
United States	590	United States	1600
Britain	238	Canada	830
Canada	200	West Germany	493
Czechoslovakia	185	Belgium	486
West Germany	183	France	425
Netherlands	180	Venezuela	378
France	170	Netherlands	368
Belgium	151	Czechoslovakia	362
Argentina	128	Britain	353
U.S.S.R.	100	U.S.S.R.	350
Japan	97	Poland	340
Chile	95	Italy	302
Italy	67	Colombia	282
Poland	60	Argentina	246
Venezuela	58	Spain	188

Table 7.4 **Radios per 1000 Inhabitants—Continued**

1950		*1975*	
Brazil	51	Yugoslavia	188
Colombia	45	Chile	175
Mexico	39	Mexico	171
Yugoslavia	29	Egypt	129
Spain	25	Japan	119
Turkey	25	Turkey	96
Egypt	16	Brazil	84
Philippines	6	Philippines	51
Thailand	5	Indonesia	17
Burma	2	Burma	12
Indonesia	2	India	11
India	1	Nigeria	9
Nigeria	1	Thailand	8
Pakistan	1	Pakistan	6
China	?	China	?

Here we find a startling increase for almost every country and for the United States a situation where there are more radios than people. (Considering the omnipresence of car radios and transistor sets, this is not implausible.) For the underdeveloped countries of Asia, Africa, and Latin America the *absolute* increase in the number of radios is sometimes great (for example, Venezuela, Colombia, Mexico, Turkey, and Egypt) but is more often fairly modest, especially for the poorer countries. Nevertheless, the *percentage* increase is usually very great, with many Asian and African countries showing a projected growth of between 500 per cent and 1000 per cent. It is hard to know whether the social and political effects of the large percentage increase will outweigh the fact that the total change is not too great, but the potential for greatly expanded mass access to modern communications is certainly there. In some cases it is even greater than these figures show. The Egyptian government, for example, has adopted a deliberate policy of installing radio and television sets in the center of small poor villages, where they can be seen and heard by all the inhabitants. Like literacy, access to a radio does not imply technical skill, but it does mean exposure to communications from the world outside the village.

Trends in Inequality

So far we have been able to look at projected changes in the rankings of various countries, and to see changes in the absolute levels of possession of goods like radios and hospital beds, but have lacked a good way of talking about our central interest—inequalities. What we need is a measure, a summary index, to say whether one pattern of distribution is more or less unequal than another. One possibility would be simply to say what proportion of the world's G.N.P. was held by, for instance, the richest 10 per cent of the world's population in 1950 and compare it with the projected distribution for 1975. That would be helpful, but it would tell us only about that single point in the distribution, the richest 10 per cent.

Another and more widely useful possibility is to make use of the *Lorenz curve* and the *Gini index*. A Lorenz curve is drawn by plotting on graph paper the points in a cumulative distribution of percentages. The poorest countries in 1950 were Burma and China. Together they held 28 per cent of the population of the world (we will here speak of our list of 30 countries as the "world," although actually they have only a little more than 80 per cent of the world's population) but less than 4 per cent of its G.N.P. We can continue this way up to all countries *except* the United States, which together account for over 92 per cent of the world's population but less than 54 per cent of its G.N.P. By connecting these points we can have a graph like Figures 7.1 and 7.2, which show the Lorenz curves for our four distributions of values—G.N.P., hospital beds, literacy, and radios—for 1950 and 1975. The cumulated percentage of population is given along the horizontal axis and the cumulated percentage of the value along the vertical axis. The 45-degree line represents the condition of perfect theoretical equality, where each percentile of the population would have an equal share in the cumulated total of the value. Thus under perfect equality each 10 per cent of the population would have exactly 10 per cent of the G.N.P., and so on. How far, in fact, the curve for a particular distribution departs from the "line of equality" gives us a visual measure of the inequality involved.

Now the Lorenz curve provides an extremely useful way of showing the complete pattern of a distribution, but it is difficult to compare whole curves for any substantial number of distributions, and it is especially difficult to interpret curves that cross each other, as the ones for G.N.P. and radios do in Figure 7.1. We can, however, measure the *area* between the cumulated distribution and line of

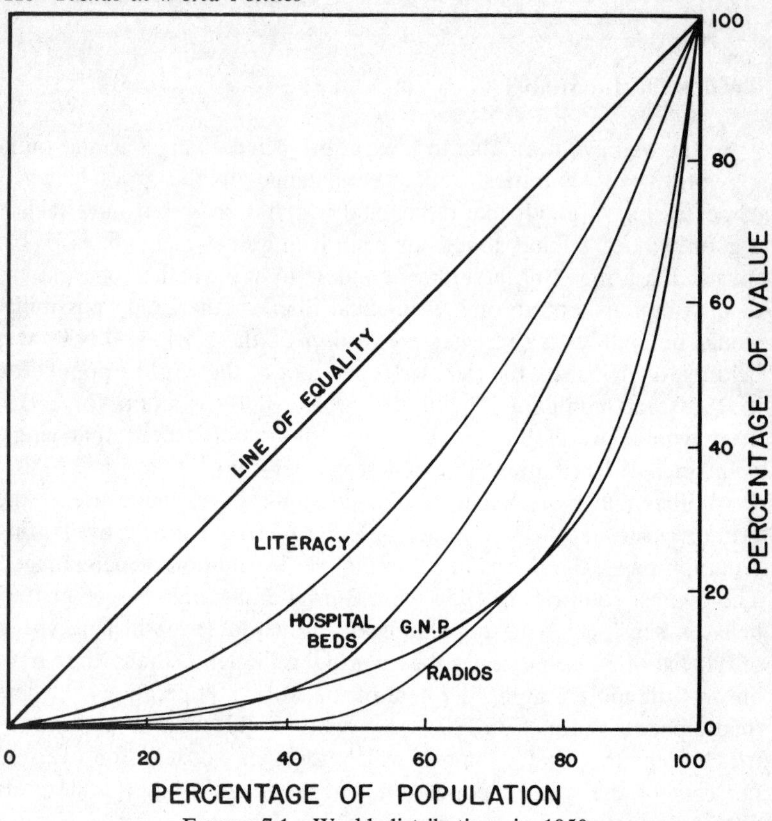

FIGURE 7.1 World distributions in 1950.

Gini Indices

G.N.P.	.66	Literacy	.30
Hospital beds	.49	Radios	.68

equality. This gives us the Gini index, a simple measure of the total inequality of a distribution. The Gini index calculates over the whole population the difference between an "ideal" cumulative distribution (where all shares are equal) and the actual distribution. The Gini index may vary from 0 to 1.0; the higher the index the greater the inequality.[4] It should be clear, of course, that use of the line of equal-

[4] The Gini number for a Lorenz curve is actually twice the area mentioned divided by the area (10,000 for 100 by 100 axes) of the whole square. The formula is

$$G = \frac{2\int_0^{100} (x - f(x))\,dx}{10{,}000}$$

where x is the cumulated population percentage and $f(x)$ is the height of the Lorenz curve.

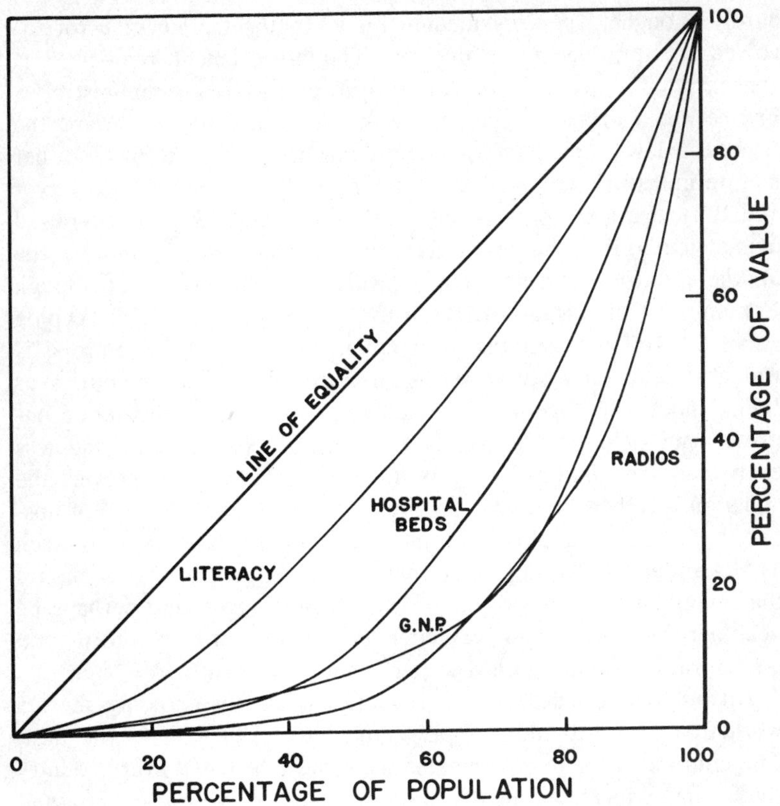

FIGURE 7.2 Projected world distributions in 1975.

Gini Indices

G.N.P.	.62	Literacy	.24
Hospital beds	.49	Radios	.68

ity in our calculation does not imply that we consider perfect equality to be a desirable goal. That is quite a different question; we merely use it because we must have some base line against which to measure real-world distributions. At the bottom of each of the graphs you will find the Gini indices for the distributions in each year. Notice how literacy is distributed quite equally around the world, but G.N.P. and radios much less so.[5]

We find a small over-all decrease in the inequality of the world's distribution of G.N.P., but only from a Gini index of .66 to .62—

[5] The curves for radios and especially hospital beds are not strictly comparable with the others, because data was missing for several poor countries and the degree of inequality is understated.

hardly enough to be very meaningful given the margin of error involved in any projection of this sort. The improvement, remember, is concentrated in two areas—Western Europe and the Communist bloc. France and Germany appear to make important strides toward the American level, and Eastern Europe reaches levels typical of rather mature industrial powers. But Communist China, and perhaps Egypt and Burma, are the only poor countries to show substantially raised living standards in these projections. In other words, though the middle countries tend to catch up with the richer ones, and though Communist China is, according to this projection, more than keeping pace, the gulf between the poor countries and those of Europe is widening, and seriously so. Such large underdeveloped countries as India, Indonesia, Nigeria, and Pakistan show only very moderate improvement, at a rate far below that of European nations and less even than the United States. With health conditions, however, the situation is rather different. The Gini index for the distribution of hospital beds remains at .49, and some of the underdeveloped states, such as Nigeria and India, appear to make the most progress. This implies that many citizens of poor countries will live longer, and perhaps be healthier, but still remain very poor. But we do not have information on several important countries, particularly Pakistan and China.

All our data on access to mass communications certainly show a world that is much more closely linked together than in the past. The Gini index for radios remains the same (.68), but every country shows major increases on the absolute index of radios per thousand inhabitants. If we assume a potential audience of perhaps four persons per radio (probably not an overestimate, at least in an underdeveloped area) even such relatively backward countries as Egypt will have over half their population regularly exposed to this modern medium. And for literacy we found not only a sharp improvement in conditions in most underdeveloped areas but even a notable decline in the already low Gini index, from .30 to .24. High levels of literacy (50 per cent or more) will very shortly come to characterize all but the poorest countries, and even they will have sizable educated elites.

In other words, some of the conditions for a revolutionary potential will be stronger than they were. Communications will be such as to make it very easy, for many poor people in backward areas, to become aware of just how impoverished they are. They will also have the means of communicating with others, both in their own countries and elsewhere, who feel themselves deprived. In this sense joint action will become possible. Furthermore, serious inequalities will persist. There will not have been enough time to modify them significantly, and in any case the trends are not in the direction of important modification in the case of the underdeveloped non-Communist states. (One important goal—better health conditions—will be much nearer achievement, however.) We cannot know whether these developments—wider communications, continued inequalities of income—will go far enough to make the danger of world conflict between haves and have-nots become really serious, but at least the risk will be higher than it was in the not-so-distant past.

Power and Revolution

The other factor that we listed as a common element in revolutionary situations was some possibility of success. Would a group of underdeveloped countries, acting together, conceivably have the power to create a situation that would be potentially dangerous for the peace and stability of the world? Here we can look again at our basic index of national power—total G.N.P. Table 7.5 shows the percentage distribution of world G.N.P. in 1950 and in 1975.[6]

Table 7.5 Percentage Distribution of Total World G.N.P.

1950		*1975*	
United States	46.4	United States	33.0
U.S.S.R.	9.5	U.S.S.R.	18.2
Britain	8.1	West Germany	7.1
France	4.2	China	7.0
West Germany	3.8	Japan	4.9
China	3.6	Britain	4.2
Canada	3.3	France	3.7
India	3.3	Italy	2.8
Italy	2.1	Canada	2.6
Japan	2.1	Brazil	2.4

[6] These figures are not strictly comparable with those in Chapter 1, because we lack the information necessary to adjust poor countries' G.N.P. estimates in terms of a common price structure. Thus the gaps are exaggerated (for example, the Soviet Union is closer to the United States, both in 1950 and in 1975, than would appear), because these give only G.N.P. at official exchange rates.

Table 7.5 Percentage Distribution of Total World G.N.P.—Continued

1950		*1975*	
Brazil	1.6	India	2.1
Belgium	1.2	Poland	1.9
Indonesia	1.2	Czechoslovakia	1.2
Argentina	1.1	Spain	1.0
Poland	1.1	Indonesia	.9
Spain	1.1	Mexico	.9
Mexico	.9	Netherlands	.8
Netherlands	.9	Yugoslavia	.8
Czechoslovakia	.7	Belgium	.7
Pakistan	.7	Venezuela	.7
Philippines	.5	Philippines	.6
Turkey	.5	Argentina	.5
Egypt	.4	Turkey	.5
Yugoslavia	.4	Egypt	.4
Chile	.3	Pakistan	.4
Colombia	.3	Colombia	.3
Nigeria	.3	Chile	.2
Thailand	.3	Nigeria	.2
Venezuela	.3	Thailand	.2
Burma	.1	Burma	.1

Some of the changes here are quite startling. China very clearly rises to fourth place behind only the United States, the U.S.S.R., and West Germany. Japan and Italy also rise substantially; Britain drops from third to a poor sixth, and India falls from eighth to eleventh place. And although the United States remains first, the gap between it and the Soviet Union changes from a relationship of almost five to one to one of less than two to one. As a group, the countries of the European Common Market fall not far short of the Soviet Union. To repeat: the rankings are more reliable than the actual percentages, which exaggerate the difference between developed and underdeveloped countries. Also, there is no reason to believe that these projections will really be borne out quite as they appear here. Those for Western Europe and the Communist nations may be too high; it is possible the one for the United States will prove slightly low. But based as they are on actual trends through 1960 they cannot be wildly out of line.

On the whole we find that the relative power position of the Communist countries, especially if they can act together, will be greatly improved. Even if China must operate alone without active Soviet support for expansionist moves, she will be very much stronger than any other Asian power or combination of Asian states. India, which many Westerners have seen as a potential counterweight to the Communist Chinese, will be dangerously inferior in basic productive resources. A slower-than-anticipated rate of economic growth for China would modify this conclusion, but not enough to provide much comfort. As early as 1962 the Chinese took great pains to demonstrate their superiority by deliberately attacking India and inflicting a serious if limited defeat on Indian troops along the border.

The threat of a major violent conflict along rich-poor lines seems much exaggerated, at least for the next few years. The non-Communist underdeveloped nations simply will not have the power to challenge the wealthier states, even if they should have the ambition. Only an extraordinarily rash leader could try, even in combination with a large bloc of such countries. (This is even more true if we remember that the non-Communist poor nations lack nuclear weapons, which adds immensely to the power disparity.) This does not mean that discontent may not seethe, for it is very likely to do so given the trends in income and communications access that we have noted. This discontent may lead to major efforts, especially within the United Nations, to make the developed states contribute greater sums in foreign aid. It may lead to public bitterness, to propaganda attacks on the rich powers, and possibly to a kind of racism. As we discussed in Chapter 4, the most dangerous political cleavages are those where class or status divisions coincide with splits based on some other factor like race.

These trends may also lead to the kind of domestic instability in underdeveloped countries on which Communists thrive. Dissatisfaction with the progress achieved by non-Communist governments may very well inspire Communist revolutions or the takeover of power from democratic leaders by the military. Often this may be justified in terms of anti-Communism, as has sometimes been the pattern in Latin America. This is not a trivial danger, for in the long run Communist control of these areas would of course pose a severe threat to the West. Nor are military rulers always the best answer to domestic Communist threats—some of the most dangerous Communist movements have followed in the wake of the eventual overthrow of military dictators. Military dictators, though they profess anti-Communism, have sometimes even made the kind of deal with the Communists by which the latter abstain from immediate revolutionary activity but are allowed to retain and even build their power bases among intellectuals, peasants, and labor unions. Both Batista in Cuba and Perez Jimenez in Venezuela were guilty of this, to their countries' detriment.

But the major threat to the peace would seem to stem from the quarter of China, either alone or, especially, as the leader of a group of discontented have-not countries. Such a group might include a number of non-Communist states, who worked with the Chinese from a sense of common desperation and inflammation fired by racist propaganda. Chinese possession of nuclear weapons, even if only in token quantities, will add to the danger. In recent years the Chinese Communists have stressed racism quite strongly in their appeal to African and other Asian peoples; they have used it even against the Russians, in order to gain control of Communist parties in many nonwhite countries. Much of the potential for this kind of conflict exists in embryo, and 1975 could well see it beginning to reach an advanced stage of development. Whether it will do so will depend largely on the ability of most poor nations to show some real improvement, at least absolute and at best relative, in their living standards; on the provision of substantial aid and a true concern from the West; and on the success of Chinese foreign and domestic policy.

CHAPTER 8

Political Consequences of Economic and Social Change

Stages of Economic and Political Development

In the last chapter we looked at some of the consequences, for the international political system as a whole, of the rates of change in various countries' acquisition of different goods or skills, like income, medical care, access to mass communications, and power. We shall now focus less on the international system than on the process of development within particular countries and some of its implications for stable and democratic government. At the end we shall return to our concern with consequences for the international system.

Several economists, including W. W. Rostow as well as Karl Marx, have suggested that there are rather clearly discernible stages in the economic development of nations.[1] The idea is by no means universally accepted; serious difficulties arise, for example, with the implication that there may be thresholds separating quite different kinds of economic activity. Nevertheless, if one thinks of stages theory not in any rigid sense but in terms of seeking to find consistent patterns and relationships among variables, it would be rash to dismiss it before a careful examination of relevant data.

After having seen the data in the last chapter it will come as no surprise that in a study of over 100 countries and colonies there was found to be a high correlation between G.N.P. per capita and such other indicators of economic and social development as the percentage of the population in cities of over 20,000 ($r = .71$), the percentage of adults literate (.80), the proportion of the population enrolled in higher education (.58), the number of radios per 1000 population

[1] See Walt Whitman Rostow, *Stages of Economic Growth: a Non-Communist Manifesto* (Cambridge, England: Cambridge University Press, 1960) for a stimulating and highly controversial set of ideas.

(.85), and the number of hospital beds per inhabitant (.77).[2] These variables, along with others like the percentage of the labor force employed in agriculture, the percentage of wage and salary earners in the population, and other indices of health and mass communications, form a cluster that tends to vary according to the level of economic development. Political life, however, is not so simple. As we shall see, there is no terribly clear relationship between economic development and democracy. Nor is the relationship very strong between per capita G.N.P. and some other explicitly political factors, such as the percentage of the population that votes in national elections (.46) or the revenue of the central government, including social security funds and public enterprises like nationalized industries (.47). There is a relationship, but the correlation coefficients are markedly lower, indicating that it is complex and much is to be explained.

Table 8.1 shows a little more about these relationships. All the political units, both sovereign nations and colonies (107), for which data could be found on most of these variables were divided into five groups or "stages" as identified by levels of per capita G.N.P., and are ranged from poorest to richest. For the sake of easy description these "stages" might be identified as "traditional primitive" societies (including Afghanistan, Burma, and much of Africa), "traditional civilizations" (primarily India, China, Pakistan, and most of Southeast Asia), "transitional" societies (Ghana, Indonesia, the Middle East, and much of Central America), "industrial revolution" societies (Eastern Europe and the U.S.S.R., Japan, Spain, Mexico, and most of South America), and "high mass consumption" societies (the United States, most of Western Europe, and the white nations of the British Commonwealth). These labels are far from perfect and in particular cases, especially for the first two stages, are sometimes quite inaccurate (Burma, for instance, surely has a higher level of "traditional civilization" than a couple of African countries whose per capita G.N.P. puts them into the second stage). Nevertheless they may be helpful as general guides to the kinds of societies usually found at the income levels identified by our stages. At the far left of the table is given the number of states (N) in each stage, though data are not available for each variable for every country; data for the last two variables in particular are often missing. The mean and the range for each stage is given for a number of social and political conditions.

[2] All correlation coefficients and data in this chapter are from Bruce M. Russett *et al., World Handbook of Political and Social Indicators* (New Haven, Conn.: Yale University Press, 1964).

Table 8.1 "Stages" of Economic and Political Development *

"Stage"	N =		G.N.P. per Capita	% Urban	% Literate	Students in Higher Ed. per 100,000	Hospital Beds per Inhabitant	Radios per 1000	% Voting	Central Gov't Rev. as % of G.N.P.
I	11	Range:	45–64	0–18	3–48	5–63	.0001–.0031	1–63	0–55	7–26
		Mean:	56	6	13	27	.0004	12	30	17
II	15	Range:	70–105	0–19	1–68	4–251	.0001–.0056	3–78	0–83	9–23
		Mean:	87	10	24	86	.0006	20	49	13
III	31	Range:	108–239	6–72	3–91	3–976	.0003–.0056	7–161	0–95	9–37
		Mean:	173	21	42	165	.0014	57	41	22
IV	36	Range:	262–794	7–82	38–99	42–1192	.0005–.0143	37–348	0–100	10–40
		Mean:	445	34	77	386	.0041	158	69	25
V	14	Range:	836–2577	30–70	96–99	36–1983	.0077–.0125	215–948	28–92	17–40
		Mean:	1330	45	98	650	.0097	352	78	27

* All data are for c. 1960. G.N.P. per capita is in 1957 U.S. dollars. Percentage urban is the percentage of the total population living in cities of over 20,000 inhabitants. Percentage voting is voters in national elections as a percent of voting-age population. Central government revenue includes social security funds and public enterprises.

catagories are not perfect

Note how for the first five variables the mean for each stage advances substantially with each higher G.N.P. level. But for the two political variables the relationship is less clear, and there are sharp discontinuities. For government revenue and voting turnout the mean for Stage V is appreciably higher than that for Stage I, but the intermediate steps are fairly indistinct, marked in each case by a reversal. The reversals, or declines at a higher stage, are not substantial,[3] but simply the absence of a clear increase is itself a notable contrast with the economic development variables. We shall discuss these variables more thoroughly later on.

The model implicit in our presentation is in some degree a "longitudinal" one, for we at least partially assume that as a country develops, as its G.N.P. rises, the values of the other indices rise. Stage III, for instance, in some way shows what a country in Stage II may look like some years hence. Clearly there are important difficulties in such assumptions. We can be sure of no uniformities in the developmental process, and conditions and technology change. Even a highly developed country would not, 30 years ago, have had a radios-per-1000 population ratio as high as that now typical for Stage IV states. A more direct and dependable method for examining stages would be to look at development data for many countries over long periods of time, to substitute longitudinal for cross-sectional data. We used some information on rates of change in the last chapter, but such data are very hard to obtain in any reliable form for long periods of time, and what is available seldom applies to more than a single-stage transition. The collection of adequate socioeconomic information in underdeveloped and developing countries is a very recent phenomenon—no one knows what Nigeria was like, in this respect, before the twentieth century. In the absence of good longitudinal data it may nevertheless be useful to use the cross-sectional information we have as if it in some way applied to development over time.

Economists talk about income "elasticities"; that is, the percentage increase in spending on some product, like food, that can be expected

[3] In cases like this it is sometimes customary to say that the differences are not "statistically significant," that is, the differences are so small, and the "sample" of countries also so small, that such differences might have occurred simply by chance. But proper use of the notion of statistical significance demands that one be talking about a randomly selected sample of individuals or countries—something we obviously do not have here, because we are discussing all countries for which data were available, and those for which there are no data are usually the most underdeveloped or most politically unstable.

from a given percentage increase in the income of a family or of a country. We can use this same concept to estimate from our cross-sectional data (if we are aware of its limitations) the amount of change in any variable like literacy or education that can be expected with a given increase in a country's per capita G.N.P. Just this kind of computation forms the basis for Figure 8.1.

Along the horizontal axis are measured the average percentage in-

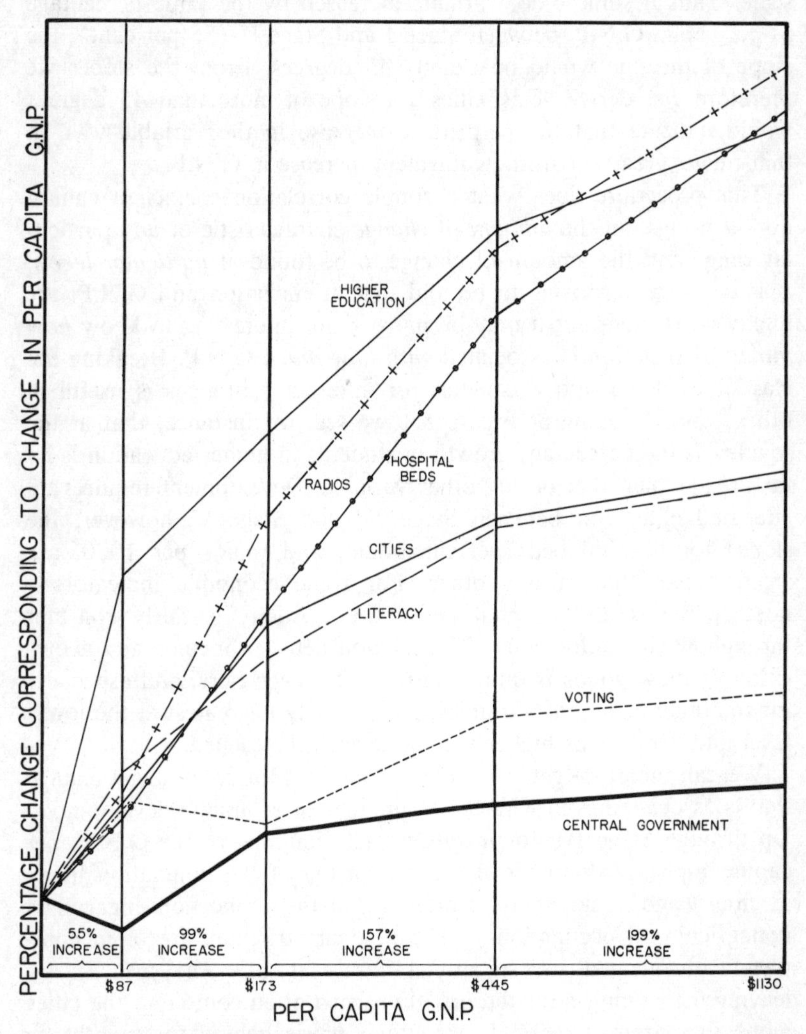

FIGURE 8.1 Income "elasticities" for aspects of economic and political development.

creases in per capita G.N.P. associated with each of the stages. Thus Stage II represents a 55-per-cent increase over Stage I, Stage III a 99-per-cent increase over Stage II, and so on. To express it differently, the vertical lines that intersect the horizontal axis represent the percentage increase in G.N.P. for each stage *over that for the previous stage,* as marked by the vertical line immediately to the left. Points on the vertical axis are placed in the same manner on the same scale. Thus if some other variable increased by the same percentage as per capita G.N.P. between Stage I and Stage II (55 per cent), the slope of the line would be exactly 45 degrees. From the slopes we therefore can derive "elasticities"; a slope of more than 45 degrees would indicate that the percentage increase in the variable was, at that range, greater than the equivalent increase in G.N.P.

This procedure does what a simple correlation coefficient cannot do—it brings out the *amount of change* characteristic of any particular range and the amount of change to be found at *particular levels.* It is not very surprising to be told that urbanization and G.N.P. are highly correlated, but it may be much more interesting to know *how much* urbanization is associated with *how much* G.N.P. Breaking the elasticities down into elasticities for different subranges is useful in other ways. Looking at Figure 8.1 we see, for instance, that at the low levels the percentage growth in students in higher education is by far greater than that of any other variable. Development requires an educated elite. But between Stage IV and Stage V, however, the slopes for hospital beds per inhabitant, and radios per 1000, are steeper than that of any other. For some economic indicators—notably radios and hospital beds—the elasticity is fairly constant throughout the entire range. The relation between income and acquisition of these goods is quite constant. But even here, and especially for the other economic variables, the elasticity is greatest at the lower level and declines as higher income levels are reached.

We can therefore get some idea of the magnitude of social change that is associated even with the beginnings of economic development. Up through Stage III, for instance, each doubling of the G.N.P. per capita implies a doubling of the proportion of the population living in cities (and, incidentally, a doubling of the proportion engaged in nonagricultural occupations). The new city dwellers are often completely uneducated and sometimes barely literate. They usually are leaving their families for the first time; men often come into the cities alone in search of work, leaving their wives behind for months or even years. Employment may be very hard to find, for there are likely already to be masses of the urban unemployed. Living conditions may be squalid, perhaps substantially worse than on the farms, and at best they will be strange. The new urban citizen must adjust to a very different way of life, to regular work at regular hours under someone else's direction. He may for the first time use money for exchange instead of bartering goods; he will be exposed, at least from a distance, to newspapers, motion pictures, and radios to a degree far greater than before. And he will be exposed to new people, new ways of life, and, in the hands of others, a kind of wealth he has never imagined. The consequences may be enormously unsettling for the social and political life of the country.

Economic Development and Political Stability

In the preceding section we remarked about discontinuities in the relation between income and political variables. They showed up both in the table and in the widely varying elasticities characteristic of different levels of development. At the beginning of the chapter we gave the correlations of several economic variables, government expenditure, and voting turnout with G.N.P. These were the coefficients for *linear* correlations; that is, where it is assumed that the relation between one variable and another remains essentially constant throughout the ranges of both variables. Linearity means that lines like those for elasticities in the preceding graph will retain the same slope at all points. For some relationships, like those between most of the economic variables and G.N.P., this assumption does not do too serious violence to the facts. But always using the assumption of linearity means frequently obscuring or distorting the true relationships, as is so clearly the case with the two political variables in the graph. It means also that the correlation coefficient computed on the basis of such an assumption will be lower than one could get by fitting the right curve to the relationship.

We can illustrate this point, as well as begin to make some useful comments about the process of political and economic development, by plotting the curve for the relation between income and central government revenues.[4] G.N.P. per capita is given along the horizontal axis of Figure 8.2, and government revenues as a percentage of G.N.P.

[4] You will notice that the scale of some variables in the following graphs, and always of G.N.P. per capita, is contracted at the upper end. It corresponds to the logarithms of the numbers shown, that is, the distance from $100 to $250 is the same as that for from $1000 to $2500. This must be done to prevent the few extremely high figures, like that for America's G.N.P. per capita—almost $2600—from contributing disproportionately to computing the correlation value.

along the vertical axis. The dots (41) on the graph indicate the position of each of 41 countries on these two variables. In addition to the curve we can also plot the line that gives the best linear fit, so as to be able to compare the two and see the improvement made by the curve.

The straight line (plotted by a method known as "least squares"; that is, minimizing the total value of the squared distances between individual points and the line) would indicate that government revenues begin as but a small share of the economy in very poor states and increase steadily with the level of development. But the curve shows that the relationship is more complex. For much of the graph we do indeed find a fairly steadily growing proportionate role of government in the economy, up to a per capita G.N.P. level of about $500. But after that it gradually levels off, and finally declines at the far right-hand side of the scattergram, where the curve drops off for the United States and Canada.[5] The curve raised the correlation coefficient to .56 from the original .47 for the linear correlation. Even so it is clear from the scattergram and the fairly low r^2 (.31) that many influences other than G.N.P. per capita would have to be taken into account in any full explanation of government activity levels. Possibly the most important thing to be learned from a picture like this is intellectual humility.

Yet the graph does tell us some useful things about this relationship, some things we could not have known from the simple correlation coefficient. Government revenues tend to be low in poor countries, where so much of the economy is subsistence agriculture. As Cubans, Chinese, and Russians have all discovered on different occasions, it is seldom easy to bring the agricultural sector of an economy very heavily under government ownership or control, and this is especially true of the subsistence farmer who produces only for his own needs, with little surplus for market. But in more fully developed states, with industry, modern communications, utilities, and a labor force that expects welfare benefits, the role of government expands very substantially. Where income levels are higher and the industrial and commercial sectors are larger, an expanded role of government is "normal"

[5] Had we used data for revenue of *all* government units instead of just *central* government, the decline would have been less, because in the United States, Canada, and Switzerland the state or provincial governments take up a larger share of the public sector than do units other than the central government in some other—and poorer—nations. Nevertheless, the basic image, including a drop-off at high levels of development, would still show even for central, state, and local governments combined.

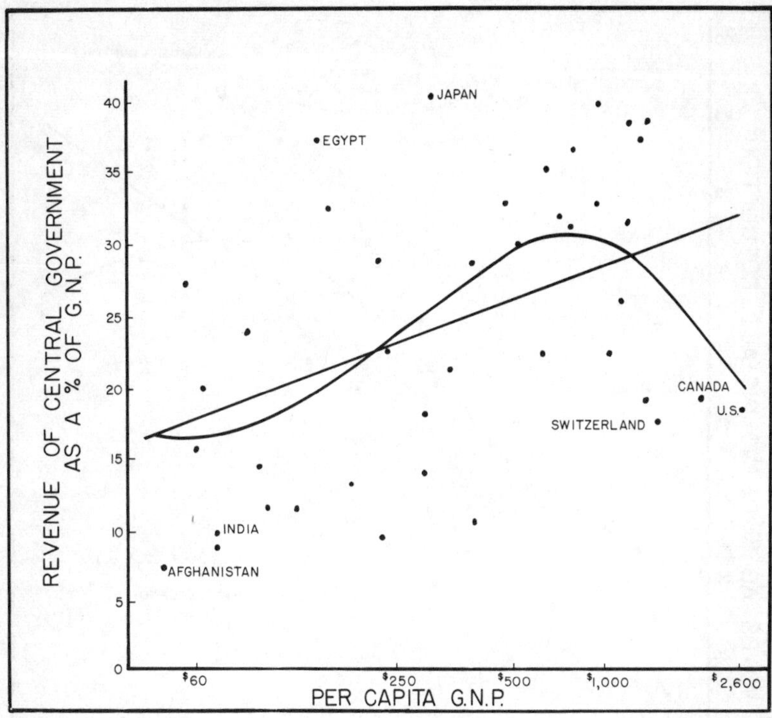

FIGURE 8.2 The role of the central government increases with economic development, but may diminish at very high development levels.

and would seem more or less to be expected—a modern economy cannot operate without substantial governmental activity.

Though there are important variations from the plotted curve, the general pattern just described nevertheless holds. No developed state, for example, shows a government revenue percentage of less than 15 per cent, although such a figure is fairly common in countries with less than $300 per capita G.N.P. But there is the curve to account for—the relative role of the public sector seems to stabilize at a G.N.P. level of around $500, and appears eventually to decline in high mass consumption societies, especially very rich states. (Table 8.1 and Figure 8.1 show the stabilization, but because the United States and Canada are averaged in with 12 other Stage V countries, cannot show the decline as Figure 8.2 does.) Perhaps a very prosperous economy can provide the necessary resources to government while keeping a constant or even growing proportion in the private sector.

Figure 8.3 shows the relation between voting turnout in national

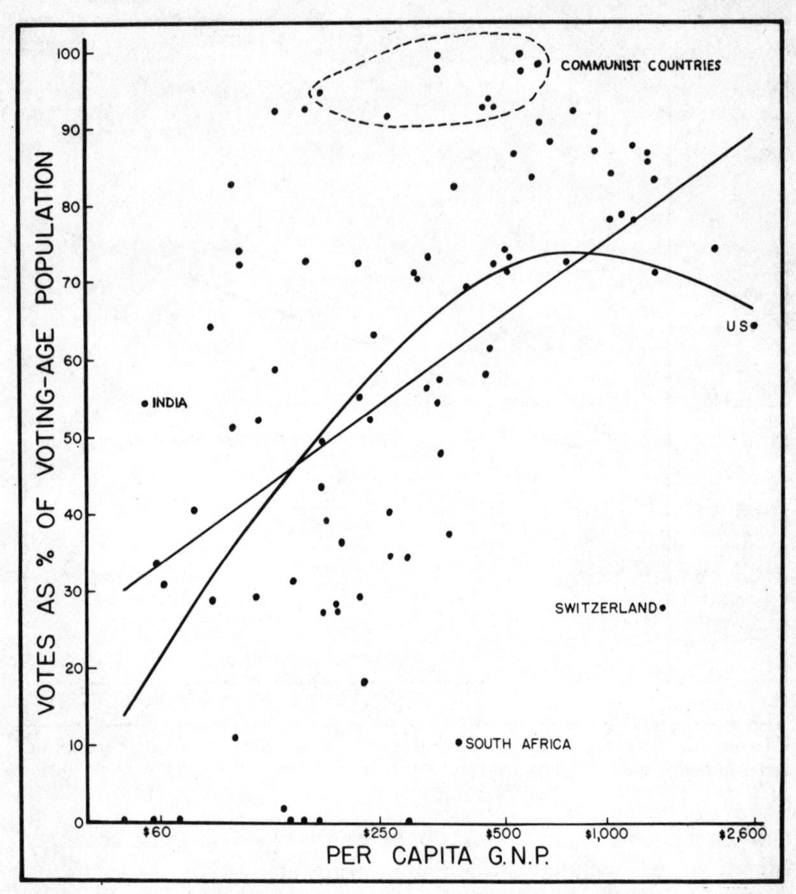

FIGURE 8.3 Voting turnout tends to be highest in developed countries, though not in the richest ones.

elections and logarithms of G.N.P. per capita, with voting percentage on the vertical axis and G.N.P. per capita again on the horizontal. We originally had a fairly high correlation (.46) assuming a linear relationship, but using a curve raises the correlation somewhat, to .51. Though there is much variation, it is clear (as it was from the table) that low voting turnout tends to be associated with low G.N.P. levels. The two tend to rise together until a per capita G.N.P. of roughly $700 is reached. (Because the curve is smoothed it does not show the temporary leveling off in Stage III that we found in Table 7.1.) After that voting levels off and even turns down again slightly with income levels of over $900. (Switzerland helps pull the curve down in the later stages because its low rate stems partly from the disenfranchisement of women, but even if doubled to 56 per cent, the Swiss figure would still be very low.)

In some degree the low voting rate for underdeveloped countries is due to states like Saudi Arabia, Yemen, and Pakistan, where elections to a national parliament have never been held—they are recorded as zero. But even in democratic countries with such low levels of income the voting turnout is not high—India, for instance, shows only 53 per cent voting, and Nigeria only 40 per cent. This is not so different from a relationship that holds *within* most countries—poor areas, and poor people in general, tend to have low voting turnout. But as we move along the scale to the middle- and high-income countries the voting rate increases sharply, reflecting one of two influences—relatively high political involvement by most of the populace in some democracies, or compulsory voting in certain states. Some authoritarian regimes even in very underdeveloped countries, like Liberia and Haiti, manage to get a voting turnout of over 70 per cent, but this is magnified in the Communist states of Eastern Europe that, without exception, achieve a voting percentage of between 93 per cent and 99 per cent. In these nations a failure to vote, without a very good excuse, is an act that may be interpreted as positive disloyalty to the regime—so it is a good idea to vote. Similarly in some democratic states (Italy and the Netherlands are examples) nonvoting makes a person subject to a fine.

Yet even without these "artificially" high instances, the peak of voting would still come for countries between $500 and $900 G.N.P. As we said, high voting rates are associated, within countries, with relatively high income and social status. But high voting rates may also be found in a population where discontent is rife, at least if the ordinary channels of political activity offer some hope of relief. This conclusion can be misleading, because it is important to emphasize the *if*. If voting is not widely seen as a politically effective act, discontent and a possibly revolutionary situation may be reflected in high absenteeism. But if voting seems meaningful and to have some potential effect, then discontent will be associated with high turnout. In the United States, for instance, voting turnout was quite high during the depression years, substantially higher than during the prosperous twenties.

Thus very high voting rates are more or less to be expected at middle levels of economic development, and they may indicate the kind of dissatisfaction and rapid cultural change often associated with fairly rapid economic development (unless they indicate one form or other of compulsory voting). The absence of reasonably high voting (c. 70 per cent?), however, may result either from an unusually high degree of satisfaction with government policies *or* from an exceptional discontent with the normal channels of political activity on the part of the populace. But widespread political activity is not typical of the early stages of economic growth, and may even decline somewhat at high levels as some people turn from political activities to their private personal lives for satisfaction.

There is more striking evidence that the process of economic development may bring important sources of tension and even violence. An index of revolutionary activity was constructed by counting the number of "deaths from domestic group violence" in particular countries between 1950 and 1962. By "deaths from domestic group violence" we mean those resulting from riots, coups d'état, civil wars, and revolutions—but not nonpolitical murders or back-street stabbings. To control for country size we made the index deaths per 1,000,000 inhabitants. Figure 8.4 shows the relation between this index of political violence and G.N.P. per capita. (Logarithms are used for both indices this time.)

The original (linear) correlation coefficient was —.43, and a glance at the graph shows why even a curvilinear fit only raises the correlation slightly, to —.47. The variation around any possible regression line is great, as most people would expect. Nevertheless, a general pattern does emerge, and its most striking feature is the low level of violence associated with high economic development (G.N.P. equal to more than $800 per capita). Furthermore, violent deaths seem to be less frequent at exremely low income levels than at somewhat higher stages. All of the nine states with G.N.P. per capita under $99 rank below eight middle-income nations in violence. There are a number of moderate-income countries with very high violent death rates, but on the average after about $200 per capita the incidence of violence declines sharply, rarely going over one death per 1,000,000 population for a G.N.P. above $800 per capita.

This picture suggests—to the extent that our cross-sectional model provides useful insights for change over time—that underdeveloped nations must expect a fairly high level of civil unrest for some time, and that very poor states should probably expect an increase, not a decrease, in domestic violence during the next few decades. In a

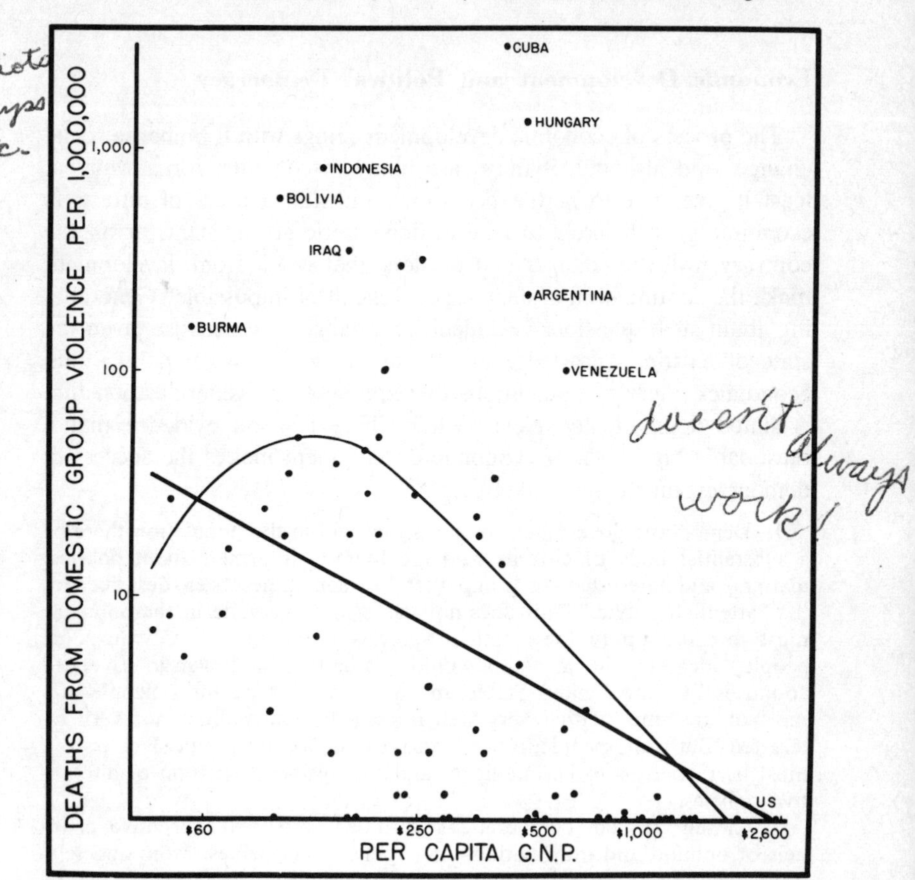

FIGURE 8.4 Political violence is associated with economic development, at least in the early stages.

traditional society knowledge is limited, aspirations are limited, and expectations as to the proper activities of government are limited—the state is not expected, for instance, to support agricultural prices, or to prevent unemployment, or to promote economic growth. All this changes with economic development. But at the higher levels of development one of three things seems to happen (probably a little of each, actually): the economic sources of discontent diminish, the ordinary nonviolent processes of government become more accessible and effective in satisfying demands, and the government itself becomes better able to control its citizens and to prevent them from resorting to violence with any hope of success.

Economic Development and Political Democracy

The process of economic development brings with it immense social change, and although it may ease many discontents, for a while at least it gives rise to new expectations and new sources of unrest. Is economic growth likely to lead to democratic government, or on the contrary, will the changes and tensions that result from development make the continuation of democracy difficult or impossible? Generalizing about such questions is difficult and dangerous, because given the state of existing knowledge about the relation between politics and economics, there are exceptions to disprove every generalization that is stated dogmatically. Nevertheless, there is good evidence that a reasonably high level of economic development makes the success of democracy much more likely.

1. Democratic government requires that within the population there be a substantial body of citizens who are literate, informed about political matters, and interested—a group that has sometimes been described as the "attentive public." This does not mean that everyone in the populace must measure up to these rather rigorous requirements; only in some people's idea of political utopia would this be true, and even in advanced countries like the United States and Western Europe most people are, most of the time, neither very well informed about politics nor very interested. But some people, other than those in formal positions of power, must be if there is to be intelligent and responsible discussion of alternative policies.
2. Closely related, democratic government requires alternative channels of opinion and information—newspapers, magazines, radio and television stations, and universities. A large proportion of these must be independent both of each other and of the public authorities, so that a variety of opinions may be expressed.
3. Also closely related, there must be diverse interest groups such as business and farm organizations, labor unions, and churches. The more such organizations there are, the more difficult it is likely to be for an individual to feel an exclusive loyalty to any one (people will be Catholics and union members and residents of a particular state or city all at once) and the more difficult it may become to drive wedges between persons who are members of any one such group and those who are not. Each of these groups will make different demands upon the larger society, demands that must be adjusted and compromised.
4. There must be somewhere for defeated political aspirants and former officeholders to go. In some cases this may mean returning to a respected and influential position as leader of an interest group; in others it may mean a position of some prestige, prospect, and affluence as a private citizen, perhaps as a lawyer. Where political defeat brings a ticket to oblivion, competition for office may become bitter.

5. Democratic government probably requires that there be other sources of enrichment than officeholding. Part of the political instability of some Latin-American countries stems from the absence of this condition. Most farmland is held in large estates—a poor peasant's son cannot hope to become wealthy through agriculture. Many of the commercial and industrial sources of wealth common to advanced countries either do not exist due to underdevelopment or are controlled by foreign companies and offer relatively meager opportunity for local personnel. Under these conditions the most available source of wealth may be government, and the result is a constant struggle for officeholding and, on taking power, the use of prerogatives primarily for the enrichment of the major political and administrative officials and their entourage—a kind of get-rich-quick approach without much thought for the broader or longer-term consequences of policy.

6. Democratic government requires reduction of the most serious *gaps* between different segments of the populace, gaps that are particularly wide because of the immense differences in outlook, interest, and life styles they represent. Examples of such gaps are those between the educated and the illiterate, urban and rural dwellers, rich and poor (where the middle class may be small), and different tribes or linguistic groups. (In an advanced society there may still be different language groups, as in Switzerland, but the educational level will be such that many people are bilingual.)

All these are conditions that can be fully met only in a country that has already achieved a rather high level of economic development. To some degree they can be provided by great effort if the leaders deliberately labor to build a democratic form of government. Sometimes also it is possible to work a democratic system even if one or more of the conditions is seriously lacking, but it is difficult, and the system's stability is likely to be precarious.

If an *existing* high level of development contributes in major ways to the maintenance of stable democracy, the *process* of development can also make a major contribution in a fairly poor country.

7. Economic development can get under way only with the emergence of new leaders at all levels of the populace. Villages that adhere to traditional leadership patterns must take new initiatives and adopt new methods—new seeds, fertilizer, irrigation systems, new initiatives in building schools or sources of power and energy. Some of the initiative must come from outside the village, but it must also come from within, and often not from the traditional leaders, who are satisfied with things as they are, but from others. Local initiative and local decision making has long been regarded as a "school" for wider activity in the democratic process.

8. The process of development can, if it appears to be meeting with some success, provide to ordinary individuals new hope for the future and new confidence in their ability to create a better life.

9. Development can provide a new goal toward which all members of the nation may strive (though of course it can also provide the possibility of sharp conflict over distribution of the new wealth).

10. Governments become regarded as "legitimate" in the eyes of their people when they solve problems and prove their ability to respond to popular needs. A successful program of economic development can provide this kind of proof.

A look at Table 8.2 will help support the argument that economic development, though it may not be *essential* to democratic government, is extremely helpful. We can use the same countries that provided the data for the "stages" table earlier in this chapter, and also the distinction between "competitive," "semicompetitive," and "authoritarian" regimes introduced in Chapter 6. "Competitive" regimes are essentially "democratic" ones. The figures in the cells show the percentage of all countries at the particular level of economic development that have a given type of political system. Percentages do not always add to 100 because of rounding.

Table 8.2 Economic Development and Political System

	"Stage" of Development				
Political System	I	II	III	IV	V
Competitive	13	33	12	57	100
Semicompetitive	25	17	20	13	0
Authoritarian	63	50	68	30	0
	N = 8	N = 12	N = 25	N = 30	N = 14

Most striking about this table is of course the absence of any kind of government, other than a democratic one, in "high mass consumption" societies. This cannot be taken too literally, because it is surely possible for such societies to have nondemocratic governments (Nazi Germany had a highly advanced economy), though they usually do not. We also find a majority of "industrial revolution" societies to have democratic governments, though this development category also includes some of the most oppressive totalitarian regimes: Communist Eastern Europe. Democratic governments are not *absent* from any of the other development groups, but neither are they *common*. Powerful forces work against the institution or continued success of democracy in these states. And democratic systems are least common, and authoritarian regimes most common, in "traditional primitive" societies and "transitional" ones.

In part these findings can be explained by our earlier discussion of the prerequisites of democratic government, but not entirely. There are several countries, which though very poor, do maintain a substantial degree of political democracy for their citizens. India, with a per capita G.N.P. well below $100, is probably the best example. But there do seem to be important reasons why the process of economic development may make it difficult, for a while, for democratic governments to continue in transitional and even "industrial revolution" societies. Democracy may not be, as an instrument for effecting economic growth, in all ways "efficient."

1. A democratic government finds it difficult to demand great sacrifices from its citizens. Totalitarian states can often, through force and repression of dissent, keep the living standards of their population very low, much lower than the people would choose if given the chance, and thus they can obtain large sums for investment. A democratic government seldom if ever can keep wages and consumption as low over long periods.

2. A democratic government finds it difficult to resist the demands for welfare benefits that are bound to be raised, in a free society, by the working class, especially in the cities. A worker who has moved from country to city gives up important elements of personal security. On the farm he was assured of a place to retire, care in time of sickness, and he was protected from unemployment. He maintained extended family ties, bonds with people who would help tide him over periods of difficulty. But the new urbanite has left the security of the farm behind, and frequently he has even abandoned many of his family ties. Faced with these new risks and uncertainties, urban workers demand pensions, unemployment insurance, and medical benefits. But providing them is expensive, and it subtracts from the already meager supply of funds potentially available for productive investment.

These first two points are rather vividly illustrated in a society that is now clearly democratic. Eighteenth- and nineteenth-century Britain underwent a tremendous period of economic and social change, in which the national income grew rapidly in the first industrial revolution. It was able to grow so rapidly because of a rather frugal class of entrepreneurs who plowed back a large segment of their profits into investment, and because of abysmal working conditions and miserably low wages, which kept profits (and therefore investment) high. It was only after several cumulative expansions of the electorate, by reducing and finally removing property qualifications, that working conditions and wages were markedly improved by trade-union activity and political reform. Until 1867 the British electorate included just a million men, none of them from the working class, and only in 1918 was universal male suffrage introduced. Economic growth was made possible, in large part, because political democracy was limited to the middle and upper classes. But in most underdeveloped countries this limitation is not possible, even if one were to consider it desirable.

Universal suffrage is virtually everywhere the rule, and the ability to enforce economic sacrifice on wage earners is limited.

3. A democratic government is often forced, for political reasons, to accept economically inefficient development plans. The Indian government, for example, decided to build an oil refinery in the state of Bihar, because the location of labor, transportation and communication facilities, and markets made that the lowest-cost area of production. Political leaders in the state of Assam bitterly contested the decision, however, contending that because the oil was drilled in Assam, and because Assam was a particularly poor state, the refinery should be there. In the end the government decided to build two refineries, one in Bihar, one in Assam. The decision was forced by political considerations that contradicted economic ones. Because it helped redress certain inequalities in the national distribution of wealth, and because it increased Assamese satisfaction with current and projected economic plans, in the end the decision may prove a wise one, maintaining Indian unity and benefiting all Indians. But it will not be an economically efficient decision, and India's economic development (excluding the effect of political factors) is likely to be just a bit slower because of it. A totalitarian regime might have withstood the political pressure (though of course this kind of pressure exists only in modified form within totalitarian systems).

For quite a while dissatisfaction with the rate of progress, with the distribution of existing income, and with the social tensions inextricably involved with great social change may result in widespread radical political activity. Despite very rapid economic growth in Italy since the end of World War II, the Communist vote has not diminished. In India it is not the poorest areas that produce the largest vote for the Communist party, but areas of relatively high literacy and even development; areas where tension, increased wants, but nevertheless a continuing deprivation produce demands for even greater change. In the long run economic development, if it benefits all segments of the population and its rewards are not confined to certain groups or classes, should deprive radical political pressure of its basic driving force. But the long run may be a long time coming.

Democracy thus encourages attacks upon itself in two different ways. First, a democratic government has a built-in handicap in its efforts to promote economic growth. It cannot squeeze its populace with the ruthless power available to a totalitarian regime, and it has to make politically expedient but economically undesirable concessions. This is not to imply that totalitarian regimes do not have their own sort of economic inefficiencies—any observer of the not-too-remote failures of the Communist Chinese could hardly think otherwise. But democracies do have disadvantages, handicaps that encourage the impatient to seek their overthrow and replacement by more "efficient" regimes.

Secondly, a democratic government is oriented toward popular participation in politics. The people are encouraged to make known their wishes and to express their grievances; that is the essence of the system. But at the same time this must be done responsibly, and the government of a developing country must walk a thin line between suppression of popular demands and permitting its acts to be nullified by local protest that contravenes the national interest.

In short, democratic rulers in underdeveloped countries are playing a risky game. On one side they face the threat of overthrow by Communists and other left-wing radicals; on the other, overthrow by "practical," "hard-headed" men of the right who would seize power sometimes to slow the pace of economic and social change, sometimes out of a fear that only a modernizing, non-Communist, but authoritarian regime can prevent leftist rule. A prospect of violence and instability faces the most conscientious democratic government in such countries. And even an authoritarian non-Communist regime will be pressed by these same social forces, it will have to resort to substantial suppression if it is successfully to control them and develop the country, and even so it may eventually be overthrown either by another group like itself or by leftists or Communists.[6]

If this seems from the viewpoint of a convinced democrat to be a bleak view, it perhaps is. Yet once economic and social change has begun in a country there is no going back, "you can't go home again." An attempt to set the clock back is the surest way to produce eventual violence and instability. And the effort to produce controlled change in an open political system is not doomed to failure, as the success of a number of countries since World War II proves. But governments determined to travel this path require aid from outside; it is virtually impossible for them to maintain from domestic sources, by democratic methods, a sufficient level of saving and investment to result in rapid enough progress. This is where economic assistance from the developed countries can fill such a crucial need.

What does this mean from the standpoint of international politics? It means that the danger of some underdeveloped countries turning Communist and becoming allies of China and/or the Soviet Union

[6] For some valuable insights see Max F. Millikan and Donald L. M. Blackmer (eds.), *The Emerging Nations* (Boston: Little, Brown & Company, 1961) and Edward Shils, "Political Development in the New States," *Comparative Studies in Society and History,* II, **2, 3** (1960).

will not pass quickly or easily. If many became Communist they could augment the power of the Chinese or the Russians. It means that these countries, if they stay non-Communist, will share important interests in terms of economic development—but it means also that they will be competing with each other for shares of the limited resources the industrial countries will be willing to make available to them. It means that economic development is likely to be a slow and not spectacular process. Too much delay could result in widespread bitterness and anti-Westernism. But it means also that the prospects for underdeveloped countries, or a group of them, becoming a united and powerful political force in world politics are limited. They may make increasing, and even increasingly successful, demands for aid, but they are unlikely to become major powers with a wide range of influence over other matters. Their G.N.P.'s will remain small, as compared with those even of the middle-level powers of Western Europe.

CHAPTER 9

Possible Future Worlds

The Decline of Bipolarity

Virtually all observers of the current world scene agree that it is changing. Few, however, agree about the depth, direction, and significance of the changes. We certainly cannot here settle the question, for the outlines are still dim and vague, but we can use the evidence in this book to make some comments about which directions seem more likely to be followed than others. Not that we have all the evidence we need or might wish; far from it. This book has been directed only to a limited number of questions, and has left others still in the realm of speculation. We have talked primarily about those trends on which there was some fairly firm quantitative evidence, especially evidence that was not widely known or not readily accessible elsewhere. Thus we are able to make statements about some trends, but merely can point out the uncertainties, and specify what we would like to know about others. Perhaps the most useful task is first just to identify where we have been and some of the possible directions in which we may be going.[1]

In Chapter 1 we identified the post-World War II system of international politics as essentially *bipolar,* with two superpowers leading alliances in direct conflict, and a numerically large but economically and politically weak portion of the world attempting to maintain a neutral, nonaligned status. During the early postwar years the United States held a *predominant,* but not *dominant,* position by virtue of its nuclear and productive superiority over the Soviet Union, but by the late 1950's the Russians had narrowed both these initial gaps.

Yet as the Russians began to catch up, other forces were working toward a loosening of the bipolarity. In G.N.P. both France and West

[1] Some stimulating reading that complements the approach of this chapter can be found in Morton Kaplan, *System and Process in International Politics* (New York: John Wiley & Sons, 1958), esp. Chs. 1–3; William H. Riker, *The Theory of Political Coalitions* (New Haven, Conn.: Yale University Press, 1962), esp. the last chapter; and Richard Rosecrance, *Action and Reaction in World Politics* (Boston: Little, Brown & Company, 1963).

Germany, the major countries of Continental Europe, grew appreciably faster than the United States, and at more or less the same rate as the U.S.S.R. Communist China did likewise, thus narrowing slightly the great gulf between the power of the United States and that of the second-level states. Britain, however, which for some time after World War II was clearly the number-three world power, slipped badly relative to China and the Continental nations. For a while Britain was able to maintain its lead over the others by its nuclear capabilities, but by the early 1960's the English had found an independent nuclear force to be expensive and difficult to keep up to date, and also found themselves no longer the only nonsuperpower with atomic weapons. France had built atomic bombs and a delivery capacity of sorts, and Communist China had created some of the appearance if not the reality of nuclear power.

Partly as a consequence of a new feeling that the United States, now vulnerable to direct and devastating Soviet retaliation, could no longer be depended upon to come to the defense of Western Europe, partly from a desire on the part of formerly powerful nations to reassert their independence after more than a decade of postwar reconstruction, serious changes occurred within NATO. Despite some fits and starts, on balance the "Six" of the Common Market seemed to be drawing ever closer together. Both in terms of political institutions and the underlying bonds like trade, they were much more closely knit in 1965 than a decade and a half before. Britain, however, seemed to be becoming more isolated from the Continent—her abortive effort to enter the Common Market in 1963 merely confirmed the judgment indicated by some of the subsurface trends. The Six also, by the same tests, were drifting somewhat away from the United States. Thus there arose the potential of a major European power, identified in culture and to some degree in interest with the United States, but having the inclination and the power (a G.N.P. not much less than Russia's) to pursue a rather independent course. This development is not, at this writing, by any means a clearly established fact, and we would need much more evidence to be sure, but important trends of European unity and insularity point in its direction. To some extent just this development had, since the Marshall Plan, been the goal of the American foreign policy, but most Americans had not envisioned quite so much independence.

A parallel trend was occurring in the Soviet bloc, though the divisions there seemed potentially deeper and more bitter. Despite their common ideology, the national interests of the two major

Communist powers diverged seriously. Throughout her long history China has alternated between domination of the surrounding territory, and being herself under the control of foreign powers. Foreigners thus were regarded either as weak and barbarous, and therefore contemptible, or powerful and domineering, and thus to be hated and distrusted. China's current rulers are Chinese as well as Communists. Though the Soviet Union was, as a fellow Communist nation, an ally, the ages-old Chinese attitude toward foreigners applied to Russians as well. Potential Sino-Soviet frictions were further fed by Czarist Russia's actions in preying (along with several Western powers) on the weakness of China in the nineteenth and early twentieth centuries, when Russia annexed vast areas of Chinese territory to Siberia. Nor were these potentials diminished in the 1920's and 1930's when Stalin advised the Chinese Communists against revolutionary activity, and when he collaborated with their enemy, Chiang Kai-shek. Stalin's argument was that China, as a peasant society, could not offer the kind of urban proletariat base needed to make a successful social revolution. The Russians, he reminded them, had made their revolution by a combination of the workers and the peasants, and in China there were just not enough workers. Marxism demanded a higher state of economic development for the revolutionary situation to be ripe. In the end, of course, the Chinese Communists succeeded even without a large urban working class to back them; theirs was clearly a peasant-based revolution. Mao and his followers could see that the Russians, as interpreters of Marx's holy writ, simply had been wrong —and Mao emerged as a major theoretician.

China is still a very underdeveloped country, and her needs and problems are often quite different from those of developed and heavily industrialized Russia; China's economic condition is appreciably worse even than Russia's in the 1920's. The Chinese expected substantial material and economic assistance from the U.S.S.R., but on the whole they did not get it. The Russians pitched in fairly generously for a while, but by the late 1950's their efforts to spread their influence in the non-Communist underdeveloped world led them to extend substantial economic aid to countries like Egypt, Syria, Iraq, Indonesia, and India. The Chinese bitterly resented Russia's decision to give this aid to non-Communist powers rather than to themselves. They were particularly unhappy that India, with whom they felt themselves to be in direct competition, should get Soviet aid while China needed it.

As an underdeveloped country China takes a different view of the gains and losses from alternative policies. The Russians emphasize the theme of peaceful competition with capitalism, saying that Communism can win without war and that thermonuclear conflict would be disastrous for both sides. The Chinese retort that only the capitalists would be annihilated, and that Communism would win in war. Now it is important to distinguish Chinese words from Chinese deeds. The Communist Chinese talk about America as a "paper tiger," but in practice they have shown remarkable respect for American military power. They have pursued a cautious (though not unaggressive) policy, attacking only weaker powers like India and Tibet, and, in the former case, calling off the attack before there was any danger of direct Western intervention. Chinese pressure on Laos and Vietnam also has been disguised and limited to aid to guerillas, a careful avoidance of anything that could call forth direct conflict with the United States. And again, Chinese military activity in the Taiwan straits has been very restrained.[2]

Nevertheless, there is probably a difference of degree between China and Russia on this point. China is underdeveloped and undoubtedly has less to lose from war than does Russia, which has so painfully built a modern industrial complex. Also, the more difficulty China has in promoting rapid economic development, the more desperately her leaders must sometimes look for some other course. But the differences can easily be exaggerated. Probably more important is that the Chinese, not surprisingly, attach greater value to Chinese interests than do the Russians. The Soviets are prepared to run greater risks in Europe (Berlin) than in the Taiwan straits. Russian failure to promise nuclear support to Mao in his 1958 effort against the offshore islands incensed the Chinese, who were convinced that given a firm Soviet stand the United States could have been deterred from intervening. This leads finally to another major irritation—Soviet failure to supply China either with nuclear weapons or with the technology to build them. Like France in the West, China felt impelled to acquire nuclear weapons under her own control, so that they, or their threat, might be used to further interests important to China, though not necessarily to the U.S.S.R.

Thus there are real and deep divisions between the two powers, divisions that may occasionally be expressed in the language of an ideological quarrel but that actually go much deeper. Though we are likely to see ups and downs in the Sino-Soviet quarrel, the nations

[2] For some evidence see Alice Langley Hsieh, *Communist China's Strategy in the Nuclear Age* (Englewood Cliffs, N.J.: Prentice-Hall, 1962).

involved are unlikely to compromise the dispute entirely, and China is certain to exert substantial independence for a long time. Meanwhile there is no denying that, despite their economic dislocations, the Chinese are deriving important benefits from independence, benefits that would be denied them as close allies of the Soviet Union. For instance, as a nonwhite power that successfully made a Communist revolution in an agrarian economy China is able to attract great support within the Communist parties of many underdeveloped countries, often splitting the parties and not infrequently coming up with the majority.

A New Balance of Power?

At the least, then, the rifts within both NATO and the Soviet bloc promise a loosening of the degree of bipolarity that characterized the 1950's. There is virtually no convincing evidence of a serious return to a tight two-power confrontation. But it is much more doubtful whether the system will change so greatly as again to resemble a balance-of-power system. A balance-of-power system requires several powers of more or less equal strength, able to shift alliances so as to counter a strong power (or powers) that has ambitions to dominate the system. It is impossible to be sure how many such powers are essential, but four would seem to be the lowest of possible minima—in a three-power system a two-against-one alliance must always threaten to degenerate into the demise of one.

No matter how independent China acts, it will be decades before she is a major world power on the level of the United States or even the Soviet Union. China has population but little else that is needed to compete on equal terms with a superpower. By any reasonable basis of comparison her G.N.P., that basic measure of productive capacity, will not exceed half of Russia's for a long time, perhaps not in this century. Furthermore, China will be deficient in most of those elements that are particularly important to great-power status—a scientific and industrial establishment capable of producing up-to-date weapons. For some time even China's nuclear capability will be more important for demonstration and propaganda purposes than as a force capable of taking on a superpower in any but the most desperate circumstances. Unless she can tap the technology and production of another power (possibly in the West?) China cannot easily build a modern delivery force.

This is not to say that China cannot or will not become a major nuisance both to the West and to the Soviet Union. She promises to have the power to squeeze and threaten all the states along her border, not excluding India. China will be a dissatisfied, revolutionary power for quite a while, and is unlikely to shrink from violence in those areas, especially on the mainland of Southeast Asia, where geography makes her strong and puts the superpowers at a disadvantage. A China with nuclear weapons, moreover, will pose a continuing risk of some reckless or desperate act. A danger, a power to be reckoned with, a loosening force to prevent a return to bipolarity—certainly. But a state capable of playing an equal role in a balance of power system—no, not for some time.

Much the same must really be said for France, acting by itself. France's G.N.P. is unlikely to exceed China's, though France will have important advantages in terms of a scientific and industrial base, and a proven if limited capability to manufacture nuclear weapons and the vehicles for their delivery. Materially, France is better suited to play the role of independent power than is China, but the gap between France and either superpower will still be enormous. In much of her recent foreign policy, especially in Southeast Asia, France really has been overextended. Furthermore, one must doubt whether, over any sustained period, France's independence and Franco-American bitterness are likely to equal what we have seen within the Soviet bloc. Though the divisive forces within NATO are real, the underlying bonds seem strong enough to prevent a full break, especially given French relative weakness.

France, in company with a united Europe, even a "little Europe" of the Common Market Six, however, would be quite a different thing. The Common Market countries together have a G.N.P. virtually equal to Russia's, and they are fully as advanced in modern technology and industry. French nuclear knowledge, put at the disposal of German science and the productive capacity of the entire Six, could produce a significant military force. Because there are important trends suggesting ever greater unity among the six, and possibly increasing estrangement from the Anglo-Saxon powers, this outcome cannot be written off as utterly implausible.

We must remember, however, that one of the key elements of a balance-of-power system is flexibility; the willingness as well as the ability to shift alliances so as to counter a power or combination of powers that threatens to grow too strong. Each power must be relatively indifferent as to which other power or powers it aligns itself with, if the result is to prevent any other power or group from dominating the system. Thus a Communist and a Western power might ally with each other to restrain another Western power, or another Communist power, or a combination. Furthermore, the winning powers in a coalition would have to refrain from pushing the defeated state to the wall, because their purpose should be to restrain it from getting too strong, but not to defeat it so badly as to remove it from the system—it might be needed again, in the future, in some other combination. They must, in short, accept limited aims.

Now given the kind of world we live in this seems just a bit far-fetched. This is not the world of eighteenth or nineteenth century, when all the nations of Europe were, for much of the time, bound together by ties of intermarriage, common interest, and a common culture. This is a world of basic ideological and cultural divisions; while ideology may be soft-pedaled at times and may seem to be being watered down, it still is with us, and keeps tension, hostility, and suspicion between Western and Communist nations high. One must really doubt very seriously that the Communists have abandoned their goal of absolute superiority (though perhaps achieved peacefully) over the West; the idea of a shifting balance and the acceptance of *permanent* coexistence with non-Communist powers does not seem very prominent even in Soviet thinking. Maybe eventually it will be, but it is not so now. Permanent coexistence probably is not envisioned by many responsible Western leaders either, at least so long as the Communist states remain Communist. Nor are the Western powers, over the long run, likely to ignore the basic cultural and commercial bonds, built up over centuries, that make them understand each other, and prefer each other, to an extent not shared by non-Western states. There are of course signs of a willingness to shift back and forth—Chinese and French overtures to each other; occasional improvements in Soviet-American relations. But at the moment to consider these as more than temporary expedients is probably to engage in a degree of wishful thinking. Eventually we may again get a balance-of-power system, but it is not around the corner.

But whatever the prospects that somehow a balance-of-power system might develop with these four units—Russian, Chinese, American, and European (probably Continental, possibly with Britain), there is even less likelihood of the emergence of a fifth power to take its place in the system on reasonably equal terms. Perhaps the most overrated possibility at present is that of a group made up of the underdeveloped non-Communist states, either acting with tightly integrated foreign policies or possibly even as a fully unified nation built up from smaller pieces. In the first place, again the basic power potential just is not there, and appears ever more distant. The major states at issue, India, Pakistan, and Indonesia, simply are not increasing their productive capacity as fast as either of the Communist powers or as fast as Western Europe. India threatens to slip substantially down the rankings.

Nor is there good evidence that a tightly knit group of such countries, which together would constitute a great power, is likely to emerge. To be very powerful such a group would have to be quite large. Even a United States of Africa, which does not seem in the offing anyway, would have a population, and a G.N.P., well under half of Communist China's. Continuing bitter conflicts between India and Pakistan suggest how remote close co-operation among South Asian states is. All these underdeveloped states share some major interests, not the least of which is the desire to promote their own economic development. To some degree this can be done by joint action to force the rich nations to devote more resources to foreign aid, but potential aid funds are limited, and what is politically, if not economically, available almost surely is less than these states' absorptive capacity. Thus the very fact of seeking the same goal is likely to bring them into competition for the scarce resources, and close identification among them seems remote.

But to say there is likely to be no major "underdeveloped power" to play a role as an equal in a balance-of-power system does not mean that the underdeveloped world can be ignored in our speculation on the future international system. On the contrary, we are likely to see increasing rich-poor friction over aid, the expropriation of foreign enterprises, and the remnants of political colonialism, especially in Africa. The African situation is particularly serious, carrying as it does all the elements of racial as well as economic and ideological conflict. The states of Africa put a very high priority on eliminating the remnants of white rule there, and in the event of violent conflict on the continent the European powers, America included, will not find it easy to apply sanctions to the whites of Southern Rhodesia or South Africa. Russian and Chinese Communists will hardly abstain from stirring the broth, however, and the invitation to Chinese antiwhite racism is obvious.

The chance that parts of the underdeveloped world may fall to the Communists cannot be discounted. As the process of economic and social change unfolds in these areas, as it must, it will bring them into periods of substantial domestic unrest, violence, instability, and vulnerability to totalitarian take-over. One of the supreme ironies of Marxism is that it was a theory about the way capitalist governments, in mature industrial economies, would become ripe for revolution, yet in practice every Communist take-over (except those imposed by the Red Army in Eastern Europe) has been in a transitional or industrial revolution economy. The vulnerability of the latter kind of state is clear, even though there are no grounds for despair about the future of *most* such states. If there are additional Communist take-overs in underdeveloped countries it would seem likely that the Chinese will prove ideologically attractive, but that China's inability to provide the economic aid essential to get a new Communist government under way may keep such states either allied to Russia or, like Cuba in the early 1960's, balancing precariously between the two.

In conclusion, extreme bipolarity is gone, perhaps for good. At the same time, a balance-of-power system, like that over half a century ago, has not been restored and will not be restored in the near future. We must look for something in between, something less familiar and for that reason less predictable. Its precise characteristics will depend on factors other than ideological clashes and comparative economic strength.

World Authority and Military Technology

One possibility is of course for a substantial increase in the power of the United Nations as a world authority, and an adequate exploration of this topic is well beyond the intentions of this book. We have not, for example, examined structural changes in the United Nations. If we had we could have evaluated the evidence of some increase in the organization's powers, especially in the field of international peace-keeping. UN peace-keeping forces, sent to Suez in 1956, the Congo in 1960, and Cyprus in 1964, suggest a more than trivial capability to deal with local wars that might otherwise spiral into great-power involvement. This could be of immense value in such tinderboxes as southern Africa, which have not yet become Cold War arenas.

We have, however, looked at the distribution of attitudes and intensities within the UN, specifically as manifested in the General Assembly. Our findings included: A single basic voting alignment, that of East versus West, is becoming more and more pervasive within the Assembly. In 1947 East-West votes were only about two and a half times as common as the next most frequent alignment (North-South); by 1961 the proportion had become five to one. Almost exactly the same proportions applied to speech making, which served as a measure of intensity. But the East-West dimension is *not* a single conflict, even though it may sometimes look that way. It is composed of a number of issues on which states' positions do vary somewhat along the East-West line; issues like the Cold War, colonial self-determination, and Palestine questions. The fact that the East-West dimension is composed of these separate subconflicts does give the various states some bargaining ability. On the whole, the trend is toward a decline in UN attention to Cold War problems and a notable upturn in attention to colonial self-determination. Because Cold War issues are probably more explosive than self-determination ones this much is mildly encouraging, but the increasing pervasiveness of a single dimension, East-West, seems ominous.

On East-West issues there is still a center group of some significance, though the trend seems to be toward a reduction in its size. At least there is no tendency for it to grow larger. It very definitely is not an intense group playing an active mediating role. And the polarization of the Assembly along lines of colonial status, democracy-authoritarianism, and economic ties of aid and trade remains high. The major exceptions where cross-pressures appear powerful are within the Asian group (where the effect is more to divide Asians sharply among themselves than to moderate the position of the group as a whole) and within the Africans (where the tendency does seem for most members of the group to hold to a middle position). Most of the hope for a sizable if not particularly intense middle group must lie with the Africans, and in large part the fulfillment of that hope depends on the avoidance of much violent conflict over self-determination on the African continent, an issue on which the Africans certainly are not middlemen. Over the long run there may be some possibility of a stable consensus-building party politics system growing up within the UN, but it is decidedly a long-run prospect that cannot be expected to carry the whole burden of international order. Some of the bitterest wars, like the American Civil War, have resulted between areas that were under a common government but did not agree on basic values. If sufficient agreement on values can be reached a world authority may be the only way to maintain world peace—but a premature effort at world government might destroy the chance for peace.

We have not in this book looked at developments in military technology, which is actually a crucial element in any prediction about future systems. A world with several nations in possession of invulnerable nuclear retaliatory forces would look much different either from a world where only two powers had such forces or where no country had them. For a while in the late 1950's it appeared that no one might have an invulnerable deterrent, that the advantages conferred by missiles upon the side executing a surprise attack might be decisive. Once the worst fears of a missile gap were passed, however, it became clear that weapons could be built so as to be highly invulnerable. By a combination of "hardening" (building protected launch sites that could survive all but a direct hit), dispersal (so no attacking missile could destroy more than one missile on the ground), mobility and concealment (as exemplified by the POLARIS underwater system) it became virtually impossible for an attacker to destroy an opponent's retaliatory force. The defender could take his time, ascertain with certainty just what kind of attack had been made upon him, and retaliate in a selective and controlled manner.

Yet in the early 1960's this type of invulnerable deterrent seemed to be extremely expensive and beyond the reach of all but the two wealthiest powers. The British tried for a while to build their own, but then abandoned the effort in favor of primary dependence on the United States either for protection or for providing them with an invulnerable deterrent in the form of a few POLARIS submarines. This development strongly favored the continuance of bipolarity in the international system.

Later, however, there were some indications that the situation might change once more. Various cheaper alternatives to POLARIS emerged, including possibly missiles aboard surface ships or simply the proliferation of Minuteman-type missiles on land, where safety might lie in numbers if not in mobility or concealment. It seemed possible that by the 1970's solid-fuel land-based missiles might be fairly cheap and within the technological capacities of several nations. Other possibilities included an aircraft fleet, of which a portion might always be kept on airborne alert and that might be able to penetrate beneath an opponent's radar defenses, delivery aboard ordinary-looking merchant ships, and, not too far in the distance, bombs in orbit.

Though the production of such weapons seemed likely to become feasible before too much more time had elapsed, the political uses to which such a "minimum deterrent" could be put were more questionable. Whether the threat to use them would actually deter the most dangerous kinds of attacks upon oneself was still an open question. They had the potential, nevertheless, of ushering in a quite different international system, one where a number of powers, not just two, had the capability of substantially destroying the productive and human resources of each other, without being able to prevent retaliation in kind. This would result in a drastic decentralization of power in the international system. It would not be equivalent to a balance-of-power system, because there would be no reason to postulate flexible, shifting alliances (alliances would be far less important than in any system in memory), and the nuclear states would not be at all equal in many of the attributes of power such as population, G.N.P., over-all military capabilities, or scientific and technical establishments. The economic predominance of two major powers, which in large part produced the original bipolarity, would remain. But a major element of the nuclear bipolarity would be destroyed, and the implications for world order would be quite different.

At this time it is too soon to know just what kind of system will emerge, or even if the situation will, in the near future, stabilize long enough for us even to be fully aware that we have a new system. But we do know that it is changing, due to changes in some of the key elements that produced the bipolar system out of World War II. We can be quite sure that it will be a world system in which all peoples will be much more closely involved than ever before. Technological trends culminating in extraordinarily rapid transportation and unimagined destructive power make it possible for modern nations to make their power felt immediately and often overwhelmingly in the most remote segments of the world, in a way that would provoke the greatest envy from a Hitler or a Napoleon. "One world" has a meaning beyond the understanding even of those who lived just a generation ago.